SCHOLASTIC'S A+ GUIDE TO GOOD WRITING

DIANE TEITEL RUBINS

SCHOLASTIC INC.
New York Toronto London Auckland Sydney

Over a million junior high and high school students have used Scholastic's A + Guides to raise their grades, do better in every subject, and *enjoy* school more. Now you can, too!

SCHOLASTIC'S A +
GUIDE TO GOOD GRADES

SCHOLASTIC'S A +
GUIDE TO GOOD WRITING

SCHOLASTIC'S A +
GUIDE TO TAKING TESTS

SCHOLASTIC'S A +
GUIDE TO GRAMMAR

SCHOLASTIC'S A +
GUIDE TO RESEARCH AND TERM PAPERS

SCHOLASTIC'S A +
GUIDE TO BOOK REPORTS

ISBN 0-590-43735-6

12 11 10 9 8 7 6 5 4 3   1 2 3/9

Printed in the U.S.A.   01

For Marc

CONTENTS

Chapter 1. GET READY, GET SET, GET YOURSELF GOING   **1**

    10 Tips to Trouble-free Writing   1

    Understanding the Assignment   7

    Hunting Down Good Ideas   9

    Narrowing the Topic   13

    Developing a Thesis   14

    Outlines: Recipes for Success   18

    Outline Warm-ups: Listing and Categorizing Your Ideas   19

    Suitable Arrangements: Putting Your Outline in Order   21

    Outlines: Compact and Mid-Size Models   22

    What's in a Name? Choosing a Good Title   24

Chapter 2. THE WRITE TIME: Getting Together the Rough Draft   **27**

    It's About Time   27

    Starting Is Half the Battle   28

    Solid Foundations: The Basics of Paragraphing   29

    Is That a Fact? Supporting Your Statements   36

    The Long and the Short of It: Determining Paragraph Length   37

    Good Connections: Making Smooth Transitions   38

Grand Openings: Catching a
Reader's Interest   42

Marvelous Middles: Keeping a
Reader's Interest   47

Exceptional Endings: Concluding
on an Interesting Note   48

Chapter 3. MATTERS OF STYLE:
Improving the *Way* You Write   51
Tone Tactics   52

On the Level: Formal, Informal,
and Colloquial Language   55

Scintillating Sentence
Structures: How to Vary Your
Sentences   57

Take Action: Using Active Verbs   59

Tell It Like It Is: The Art of
Being Specific   60

Shades of Meaning: Recognizing
the Connotations of Words   63

Nobody Speaks ''Jargonese'':
Avoiding Confusing Words   65

Shortcuts: A Guide to Plain
Talking   67

Avoid Clichés — Like the
Plague!   69

Be Consistent   71

Are You Game? Painless
Vocabulary-Building Ideas   73

Chapter 4. FINAL TOUCHES:
Editing, Rewriting, and
Polishing   75
    Tricks of the Trade   78
    You Be the Judge: Composition
    Checklists   80
    Last-Minute Mechanics   83
    Spelling Demons   84
    Punctuation Pointers   87
    Many Happy Returns:
    Understanding Your Teacher's
    Comments   93

Chapter 5. WRITER'S CHOICE:
105 Ideas for Every Kind of Paper   95
    Picture This: Descriptive Writing   96
    What's the Story? Narrative
    Writing   98
    Facts of the Matter: Expository
    Writing   100
    Powers of Persuasion:
    Persuasive Writing   103
    Test Patterns: A+ Essay Test
    Tips   106
    On the Books: Creative Book
    Report Ideas   109
    Charting a Winning Course: A
    Progress Chart for Compositions   114
    Afterthoughts: A Personal
    Record of "Write" Ideas   120

Chapter 1

GET READY, GET SET, GET YOURSELF GOING

So you have to write a composition. How do you get an idea? How do you put words down on paper? How do you make it readable? And . . . how in the world do you get an A+? With keen observation, careful planning, awareness of structure and style, plus real time and effort, it *can* be done. But if you're in the middle of a creative energy crisis of your own, read on. Good news, in the form of this book, has arrived to help.

10 TIPS TO TROUBLE-FREE WRITING

1. Think positively. The first thing you should do when approaching any school assignment is to take a deep breath and say, "I *can* do it!" Nothing, but nothing, is ever gained by screaming, crying, or tearing your hair out (except maybe a sore throat, swollen eyes, and a bald head). *Positive thinking* is a powerful psychological theory that works — not an old wives' tale or some voodoo superstition. If you feel confident that you can do something, more often than not you will. Just keep in mind that old saying, "Where there's a will, there's a way." Well, if you start by developing the will from within, you can use this book to help you to perfect the way.

2. Find a quiet place to work. Find a quiet corner in which to do your writing. If you're the kind of person who can think clearly with the stereo playing, the TV droning, and the dog barking, then congratulations, because you are in the minority. But, if you're like the majority of people who need an atmosphere that is relatively free from distractions, then it is up to you to find or make one.

If you can't resist glancing at the television set, then don't work in a room where TV is the main attraction. The same goes for a radio, stereo, or even in some cases, the refrigerator. Know what your weaknesses are and *stay away from them*!

If you share a room with a brother or sister, see if you can arrange a specific study time for the two of you. Try to agree upon a time to be used strictly for schoolwork when you both promise to be as quiet as possible, giving one another the opportunity to work undisturbed. If a time cannot be mutually agreed upon, perhaps you can go to bed half an hour later, or get up half an hour earlier in order to work.

3. Acquire self-discipline. Don't just sit back and talk about doing something — do it! No one can expect a good grade on anything that she or he threw together in minutes. Sure, there are some cases of kids who dash things off the night before and get A's, but be assured that these instances are rare. Much more common is the "night-before-it's-due-paper" that just skims by with a decent grade.

If you have a paper to write, don't squeeze it into your schedule between cheerleading practice and the Saturday night movies — *make a specific time for it.* If you must, make a list of priorities to help you organize your time better. Many of the C papers of this world would have been A's if only their creators had taken the time to revise and rewrite and think about them a little bit more. If you hurry to do something, be aware that you are cheating yourself out of doing the best possible job.

4. Stock up on supplies. Invest some of your money in a good supply of paper, pens, and pencils to keep at home. One of the absolute worst excuses to give any teacher (right behind "My dog chewed it up!") is that you ran out of paper, or couldn't find a sharp pencil or a pen that worked. Save yourself the embarrassment of having to use such a poor excuse and buy enough supplies to last at least one semester. School supplies don't spoil with time and they never go out of style.

5. Learn to type. Most teachers have not taken

a course in handwriting analysis, nor should they be expected to do so. They are not usually interested in how you dot your i's or cross your t's, but are interested in being able to tell the difference between an "i" and a "t." Teachers want, need, and expect neat, readable papers, and a sloppy, unreadable mess is grounds for a poor grade.

A typewriter is best for long writing assignments. Learning to type will be one of the most useful things you can do. This skill comes in handy in situations outside of school as well as in. If your school or community center doesn't offer typing classes, then you can buy (or borrow from a library) a self-teaching typing book that comes with records or tapes to guide you. If you can't afford to buy a typewriter of your own (and many second-hand shops and *Penny Saver* newspapers advertise great buys on used ones), then see if you can borrow one from a friend or arrange to use one in school during off-hours.

A typewritten paper won't guarantee an A+ paper, but it will be a welcome sight to the sore eyes of an English teacher who has graded 30 papers and comes upon a neat, easy-to-read 31st.

6. Apply for a library card. One of the best things in life is really free. In most communities, a library card is yours for the asking (with proper identification), so why not take advantage of the opportunity to own one? Library facilities range from books and periodicals to microfilm, records, tapes, and photographs, and can help you with almost any type of school assignment, in addition to providing an atmosphere conducive to studying.

Make it your business to get personally acquainted with your school or local library facilities and with the staff who maintains them. It will be much more fun to wander around the library and learn what it has to offer when you have some free time, rather than when you are working frantically under the pressure of an assignment.

7. Read, read, read . . . Reading what others have written is one way of increasing your vocabulary and seeing how professional writers use words to clearly express ideas. Read everything — newspapers, magazines, books, journals, billboards, boxtops, and bumper stickers. If you run into a word that you don't know, look it up in a dictionary and commit it to memory or use it in a sentence. If in your reading you train yourself to become aware of what is considered to be good writing, you will be amazed at how easy it will be to recognize bad writing — yours or anyone else's.

8. Keep a journal. Why wait for a specific writing assignment from your teacher to inspire you? Why not keep a notebook or pad of paper handy for ideas that come to mind every or every other day? Try to make it a habit to write for five or ten minutes a day on anything that comes to mind. This journal doesn't have to be like a private diary — it can merely be an organized place to record bits and pieces of ideas that may prove helpful on a future theme or report. Things such as jokes, observations, questions, quotations, anecdotes, new words, favorite poems, snatches of memorable (or even overheard) conversations, ideas for stories, news items, and character sketches are all journal material. If you do start a journal, don't feel that you must write in it every night. Let it be something you look forward to doing for fun, and don't let it become a chore.

Give journal-writing a try. And to show you how easy it is to get started, there's a journal just waiting for words on page 120.

9. Brainstorm. Sometimes you need to talk to other people about ideas that are brewing in your head. Brainstorming with a group of friends before beginning a writing assignment can be a creative and rewarding experience. Getting together with a small group of friends is a good way to get feedback on some of your ideas and a great place to give and get *constructive* criticism. If two or three of you come up with similar ideas for a paper, then work it out to write the paper from two or three different angles.

10. Buy a dictionary and a thesaurus. Two of the most useful books a writer can own are a dictionary and a *thesaurus*. (Look up the proper pronunciation in any dictionary!) You don't have to keep one under each arm as you write, but it is advisable to keep them both nearby.

If you are a bad speller it doesn't have to affect your grade — if you play it smart. One of the major advantages of a dictionary is that all the words in it are spelled correctly. So, when in doubt, look it up. (Many professional writers have admitted to having spelling problems, so be assured that you are not alone.)

If you have used the adjective "wonderful" ten times in one paragraph, you are greatly in need of a thesaurus. This handy reference book will provide you with interesting substitutes or synonyms that you can use in place of the over-used "wonderful," or any other old stand-by word that could use a rest.

Here are the titles of a few good, low-cost paperback editions of these valuable books. (Or ask your teacher for the names of ones she or he might recommend.)

American Heritage Dictionary
The Random House Dictionary
Webster's New World Dictionary
Roget's Pocket Thesaurus
Dictionary of Synonyms
      and Antonyms (Popular Library)

UNDERSTANDING THE ASSIGNMENT

It's a mistake to walk out of a classroom without completely understanding the assignment that your teacher gave you. Too often a D or an F paper staring back at a stunned student is because she or he misunderstood exactly what was expected. Yes, it's the teacher's responsibility to thoroughly explain an assignment, but it's *your* responsibility to come up with any questions that, when answered, will clear up any confusion you might have.

When it comes to asking questions, remember these tips:

1. Don't *ever* avoid asking a question for fear you'll sound stupid. Most likely, if you are confused, everyone else is as well and will silently thank you for speaking up. If shyness is a problem, however, wait until after class is dismissed and ask the teacher your question privately.

2. Don't sit and wait for someone else to ask a question that you'd like answered. You might be waiting a long, long time. And just because someone doesn't ask the question you have in mind doesn't mean that it's trivial or unimportant. *Anything that you don't understand is important.*

3. Don't expect your teacher to be a mind reader and know what you would like further explained. She or he may have a hard time "reading" the looks of over 30 faces, and it's just possible you may look like you really do understand something when, in fact, you're in a fog.

4. Before you leave the class make certain that you know the answers to these basic questions:
    1. What is the purpose of the assignment?
    2. What *exactly* am I to do?
    3. Must I type my paper or can it be handwritten?
    4. How long should the paper be?
    5. When is the paper due?
    6. What is the penalty for a late paper? (This knowledge should keep you on time!)

HUNTING DOWN GOOD IDEAS

What to write about is often the chief problem faced by many students when they receive an assignment. Sometimes a teacher will offer broad topics as possible ideas, but even then it is still up to the student to go from the general to the specific.

What should you do when your teacher ends class with: ". . . and you may write on any topic of your choice"? How does a person go about getting ideas? Try the following routes beginning with . . .

1. Don't panic!

2. Use your own experience. Luckily (or hopefully) you haven't spent your life in a soundproof booth with no windows, doors, or any contact with the outside world whatsoever. Living in such a situation would be about the only acceptable excuse for not having anything to write about — except, perhaps, "Life in a Soundproof Booth."

It is vital to your writing that you learn to observe the world around you with a fresh, alert eye. Look at familiar scenes with the awareness of seeing them for the first time. Try to train your eyes to act as a camera and your ears to act as a tape recorder. As you practice this you will soon become skilled at "photographing" and "recording" meaningful impressions in your mind. When an assignment rolls around you can draw on your memory of these experiences or, if

9

you've started a journal to store a written record, you can get an interesting idea as effortlessly as rereading your notes.

If you are now saying, "Well, that's a good idea for people who travel a lot, have a lot of free time, or extra money to do really *exciting* things," you are trapping yourself in what has come to be known as the but-nothing-interesting-ever-happens-to-*me* excuse. Give yourself more credit than that! Even simple, everyday activities can make interesting papers if you work at it. How about a serious essay on the advantages and/or disadvantages of school cafeteria food? Or a humorous piece on the "art" of cleaning your room? Or bathing a dog? Or making a salad? Creativity has no set rules and no limits (except, perhaps, those set by your particular teacher). So, if you can make brushing your teeth sound interesting, then do it.

3. Use other people's experiences. Listening and talking to other people is something you do all the time. But this type of interaction has become so automatic in some of us that potential writing ideas probably just fly by. Around the time of an assignment, why not make a special effort to pay attention to the people around you and what they have to say? Talk to fellow students, your parents, your teachers, your friends, and anyone else you can strike up a conversation with. Talk to them about a particular assignment. Exchange views. Perhaps they can offer valuable insight or interesting topic ideas. You don't have to be formal about these discussions, but you might want to ask a specific question you have in mind. You'll probably be surprised with the way other people can provide such inspiration.

Information that comes from other people is worth taking the time to investigate. Treat it like a recipe being passed along from cook to cook. Add a drop of this or take out a pinch of that, and feel free to substitute various ingredients, turning the recipe into your own prize-winning dish.

4. Read newspapers and magazines. One of the best sources of food for thought is the printed word. And those of you who want to stay on top of *all* your classes should make it a habit to keep up on the latest events through reading (and *not* just by watching TV!). Even if you are not ordinarily interested in news stories, make it a habit to at least scan these various publications for composition ideas. You'll find that current events is just one of the hundreds of subjects you'll find in print. Everything from beauty tips and health reports to movie star gossip and film reviews is written up somewhere. There is probably no subject so odd that there is nothing written about it.

If you have no access to a variety of magazines or newspapers, go to your neighborhood or school library. There you'll be able to find thousands of ideas literally at your fingertips. Browse around for a while and if you find an interesting article or news item that you want to investigate more thoroughly, you can look in the subject-card catalog or in the *Readers' Guide to Periodical Literature* for more specific information.

P.S. While you're there, don't forget to apply for your own library card. Remember that it's free and will certainly come in handy.

5. Use TV, radio, and films as inspiration. While you're letting the different media entertain you, let them help you with your schoolwork as well. You can do this by simply thinking while you're watching and/or listening. Analyze one of the characters in your favorite situation comedy. Do further research on the topic presented on *60 Minutes* or *Good Morning America*. Use a dramatic storyline as a springboard to an original essay. Does the type of gadgetry used in James Bond films really exist? Find out. Discuss how the horror or science-fiction movies of today compare with those filmed 30 years ago. Is there a story in that latest number-one hit song? Why would anyone want to be a disc jockey?

These are only a tiny fraction of the types of composition ideas that can spring from your everyday contact with the media. Learn to turn an ordinary activity into a rewarding and interesting experience.

If you are still complaining that you can't think of a single thing to write about, you are simply blinding yourself to the ideas that are all around you. The trick is to recognize them for what they are. Don't be afraid to reach out and try something new or make something new out of something old. Surprise your teacher and yourself with a topic to replace "My Summer Vacation" or "My Favorite Person."

NARROWING THE TOPIC

Once you've decided upon a topic for your composition you have to concentrate on narrowing it down to a controllable size. By doing this you will save yourself time, extra work, and most of all, frustration.

Papers dealing with "A History of Dancing," "Crime Prevention," or "Sports Heroes" are good topics but not A+ material because they are far too broad to be adequately covered in one paper. First of all, a complete history of dancing could take you years to thoroughly research. In the second instance, you could write an entire book on crime prevention and still overlook many aspects of the subject. And, finally, you could write a twenty-page paper about *baseball's* heroes alone without even touching on the heroes of all the other sports that exist.

Learn to break your topic down. If dancing interests you, why not develop a paper about one particular aspect of dancing — ballet, tap, or disco. Better yet, why not an essay about the influence one of these dance forms had on the clothing or film industry. Crime prevention can be broken into subheadings emphasizing different aspects of the topic, such as helping teenagers go straight or training the elderly in self-defense. The subject of sports heroes can be personalized to include your favorite sportspersons or turned into a report on the huge salaries today's sports stars demand. Whatever the assignment, with a little more thought, each of these three subjects can be trimmed and adapted to fit the bill.

Here are two tips about narrowing your topic:

1. Choose a topic that is both interesting and practical. Don't begin writing about something that has the danger of becoming boring to you after just a few hours of working on it. Also, try to choose a topic that you know something about or can research in a reasonable amount of time. In other words, know your limits regarding interest and time.

2. Don't try to do the impossible. Many of the subjects that students decide to tackle cannot be adequately covered in a full-length book! Focus your topic so that it can be intelligently discussed in the number of pages you are aiming for. If your teacher doesn't give you a minimum or maximum number of words or pages, give yourself a rough estimate or goal. Be realistic and take into consideration the time allotment and subject material. Certainly your writing will benefit.

DEVELOPING A THESIS

Once you've cut your chosen subject down to a controllable size, it's still not time to start writing until you decide what direction your paper is going to take. What is it you would like to say about this topic? You can't go into everything you know about it — that would be both dull and time-consuming.

For example, suppose you decide on the general subject of *food* and reduce it in size as follows: *food — fast food — fast-food chains*. Well, what *about* fast-food chains? Before you begin writing you must take one more step and convert the subject into *an idea about the subject*. For example: *"Fast-food chains offer nutritious meals at convenient, low prices."* This statement or point of view toward the subject is called the "thesis." It will provide a guideline for what you should and should not include in your paper.

The thesis of your paper should state what the topic is and show your intention. Its purpose is to keep both you and your reader on the track by helping you to organize your material and your reader to follow your train of thought — knowing in what direction you're taking him.

Here are five points to remember when developing a statement of purpose or a "thesis" sentence:

1. Write a complete declarative sentence that reflects your point of view. Don't write your thesis in the form of a question, phrase, or word.

2. Write a thesis sentence that is somewhat open to argument, rather than a self-evident fact (e.g., "Fast-food chains offer nutritious meals at convenient, low prices" [somewhat open to argument], rather than, "Many people eat at fast-food chains" [known fact]).

3. Write a thesis sentence that is somewhat open to argument, rather than a simple statement of personal preference or observation with which no one can disagree (e.g., "Any teenager who's ever been in love will enjoy *Romeo*

15

and Juliet" [somewhat open to argument], rather than, "I loved the play *Romeo and Juliet"* [simple statement of personal preference]).

4. Write a thesis statement that is limited in scope, one that covers only what you want to discuss in your composition. For example, the thesis "Fish make terrific pets" is too broad. Will you really discuss *all* types of fish? *All* ways that they make good pets? Probably not. A better thesis would be: "Goldfish are terrific, easy-to-care-for pets." This more limited thesis lets your reader know she or he will be reading about goldfish as easy-to-care-for pets.

5. Be creative. Sometimes it takes a little more thought and a little more time to come up with a new angle on your subject. But it'll be worth it. Not only will you have more fun writing about an interesting and original topic, but your teacher will enjoy reading a paper with a fresh, different outlook.

Here's a visual trick to help you learn how to narrow your subject down to a manageable size and to formulate a good thesis as the basis of your composition. Before you begin writing, think of your subject as a target. The outermost circle represents a very general subject — too broad to be handled in a well-formed paper; the next ring represents a slightly narrowed approach; and the next smaller ring represents a precise and limited topic. The innermost circle — the bull's eye — represents your point of view or "thesis."

Target Practice: From General Subject to Specific Thesis

Sports Heroes

Baseball's Heroes

Babe Ruth

There'll never be another Babe Ruth.

Dancing

Disco Dancing

Disco Dance-related Injuries

Disco injuries can be prevented.

Crime Prevention

Methods of Crime Prevention

Self-defense Courses

Self-defense courses should be free to the elderly.

OUTLINES: RECIPES FOR SUCCESS

Following a recipe is a mystery to Sheryl X. Whenever she cooks something it is totally hit or miss. Oh, she does okay with tea and toast, but when it comes to something more exciting like a chocolate soufflé, Sheryl is definitely in need of help.

"Sheryl," one honest friend finally dared to say, "this chocolate soufflé is the absolute worst!"

"I know," Sheryl answered sadly. "But I just don't understand why."

Maybe you're familiar with a similar sense of failure when it comes to your writing. And maybe you, too, don't understand why nothing seems to come out right. Oh, you might do okay with simple sentences and very short paragraphs (like Sheryl manages with tea and toast), but when it comes to a longer, more involved piece of writing, you just can't seem to get it together.

Sheryl's trouble could have been avoided if she had used a recipe. It would have helped her to see, step-by-step, how to make an edible soufflé. And don't think that recipes are just for beginners either. Experienced and confident cooks let recipes be a basic guide and adapt or change them to suit their (or their guests') particular tastes.

Any trouble you might have with writing can be avoided by a kind of recipe or outline that you create for yourself. An outline should list, in a logical and orderly manner, everything that you want or need to include in your paper. You'll probably find that a good outline will help you get facts and ideas straight before you begin to write. And, whether you type your outline formally on a piece of typing paper, or scrawl it informally on the inside of a gum wrapper, an outline will give you a sense of order and keep your next composition from being a hit-or-miss experience.

OUTLINE WARM-UPS: LISTING AND CATEGORIZING YOUR IDEAS

The first step toward creating a workable outline is to *list all your ideas related to the thesis of the paper.* At this point you shouldn't worry about the order of your ideas or whether you will even use them all in your final paper. Just force yourself to jot down everything you know or think you can use in a paper on your chosen topic. (For some reports this list may include some information you've gotten by doing some research.)

Here's an example of what a list of ideas (or composition "ingredients") might look like if you were going to write a paper on the topic of "Education," with your thesis being, "Getting a high school diploma is the most important thing you can do."

1. get a better job
2. make more money
3. have greater self-confidence
4. gain respect from others
5. improve basic reading, writing, and math skills
6. make good friendships
7. win confidence of others
8. impress family and friends
9. get invited to the senior prom
10. qualify for college
11. learn to accept greater responsibility

Notice that there is no order to this list. The items are simply ideas that might occur in your head as you think about the thesis statement. In this case, the ideas are all reasons explaining "why?" (If you were comparing two things, such as high school graduates and non-graduates, you would have two lists of ideas.)

Once you have thought through all the possible ideas related to your thesis and listed them on paper, the next step is to order or *organize* them into a useful outline from which you can begin writing. In order to do this you must first group your ideas into common categories and eliminate any ideas that don't fit into your plan, either because they are unrelated to the subject or, if included, would make the composition too long. For example, in going over this list, you might decide to eliminate #6 and #9 because they both are related to the social aspects of high school that you decide not to discuss. This leaves you with nine items remaining that could be grouped as follows: Items 1, 2, and 11 all deal with job benefits. Items 3, 4, 7, and 8 all deal with character and personality benefits. Items 5 and 10 deal with academic benefits. Basically, this grouping is an outline. All you need now is the proper form.

SUITABLE ARRANGEMENTS: PUTTING YOUR OUTLINE IN ORDER

Once you've identified categories for your items and eliminated the unwanted ideas, you need to choose a logical arrangement for your reasons, facts, or examples. Here are some of the numerous methods of arrangement you may choose from:

1. Chronological (time) order
2. Order of importance
3. Spatial order (from place to place, near to far, left to right)
4. Comparison and contrast
5. General to specific

The order thought to be most effective for this sample outline consisting of reasons supporting the thesis statement ("Getting a high school diploma is the most important thing you can do") is *order of importance*. The decision, of course, is up to each individual writer. What must be considered is fulfilling your purpose and satisfying your reader at the same time.

OUTLINES: COMPACT AND MID-SIZE MODELS

The Topic Outline

Probably the easiest and clearest outline to make and understand is the topic outline. Each item listed is simply a topic to be discussed in the paper and is *not* a sentence. For most of the outlining you will do for school assignments, the topic outline should be quite adequate unless your teacher prefers a more detailed plan such as a sentence outline provides.

The Sentence Outline

A sentence outline uses what its name implies — complete sentences. It is always clearer than the topic outline because it gives more details about the meaning of each topic mentioned. If you have a poor memory, you might find a sentence outline more desirable.

Here is a comparison of the topic outline with the sentence outline. Study the form and detail of each, noting that every main heading must have at least two subheadings. Adapt whichever you are more comfortable with when it's time to outline your own paper, keeping in mind that they are both correct and acceptable (unless your teacher specifies otherwise).

Topic Outline
  I. Personal Benefits
      A. Greater self-confidence
      B. Respect and confidence from others
      C. Impress family and friends
 II. Academic Benefits
      A. Improve basic skills
      B. Qualify for college
III. Career Benefits
      A. Better job
      B. More money
      C. Greater responsibility

Sentence Outline
  I. A high school diploma provides personal benefits.
      A. A person gains greater self-confidence.
      B. A person gains respect and confidence from others.
      C. A person impresses his/her family and friends.
 II. A high school diploma provides academic benefits.
      A. It improves basic skills, such as reading, writing, and math.
      B. It may qualify you for college.
III. A high school diploma provides career benefits.
      A. It can help you get a better job.
      B. It can help you make more money.
      C. It can qualify you for greater responsibility.

WHAT'S IN A NAME? CHOOSING A GOOD TITLE

Once you've chosen a topic, narrowed it down, developed a thesis, and produced some sort of outline, you should take the time to think of a working title (it can be changed later if you come up with one that's more interesting — that's why it's called a "working" title). Many students find that thinking of a good title *before* beginning to write is inspirational. For one thing, it provides a sense of accomplishment and, for another, a good title can give you direction and help to bring your subject into sharper focus.

Although a terrific title cannot magically turn a frog of a paper into a prince, there is no reason to settle for less than your creative best. The title is, after all, the first thing your readers see, and you want to arouse their interest, not lull them to sleep.

Think of how boring life would be with meals consisting only of bread and water and you'll have some idea of how your teacher feels sitting down to read a pile of compositions all with titles like, "Book Report," "Summer Vacation," and "I Hate Television." These titles, like a diet of bread and water, are adequate, but very, very dull. It's hard to stifle a yawn before reading even one word.

Why not put your imagination to work and attract readers with titles that are flavorful and different. Rather than a (yawn!) title like "Dieting" for an essay on coping with the frustrations of losing weight, you could call your paper, "Don't Be a Sore Loser." A composition about your summer job as a lifeguard could be titled, "Sitting Pretty" instead of (yawn!) "My Summer Job."

Titles frequently fall into three different categories. It's your decision as the writer to choose the one that suits your purpose.

- **Summary titles** are those that provide the most general information. By giving facts without details they lure the reader into the paper if she or he would like to know more. Newspaper headlines are frequently good examples of these kinds of titles: "Hurricane Hits Florida Coast," "Sunset Concert Series Starts Saturday," and "*Star Wars* Breaks Box Office Records."

- **Preview or Give-a-Glimpse titles** aim to create reader curiosity. They introduce the subject by attempting to grab a reader's attention with a question or thought-provoking statement like "If Shakespeare Were Alive Today," "Why Won't Disco Disappear?" or "Where Will You Be in 2001?"

- **Teasing or Whimsical titles** leave your reader guessing about what's to come. They usually refer to the subject indirectly and make readers curious enough to read on. These titles can be fun for both the writer and the reader, although you might want to include a subtitle under the teaser to avoid any confusion. How about something like "Good Morning, Sunshine" (subtitled

"Solar Energy in Our Town") or "Boiling Water and Opening Cans" (subtitled "My Turn to Cook").

A striking title, whatever the type, can only work in your favor. Just be certain that it is not misleading. A good title should *honestly* lure the reader into the rest of the paper and not promise more than it will actually deliver. (Several newspapers and magazines are noted for sensational-type headlines. This practice of selling a product by exaggerating what's in the copy only serves to anger and alienate readers and is *not* a recommended example to follow.) Here are some things to keep in mind when you're trying to think of a good title:

1. Consider the material. The title should be related to the central idea or thesis of your paper.

2. Consider the audience. Will your readers understand a serious, technical title? Will they appreciate a humorous or clever title?

3. Consider the wording. Pick your words carefully, thinking of how they sound as well as what they mean. (Rhyming, alliteration, and onomatopoeia can prove interesting if used cleverly.)

Chapter 2

THE WRITE TIME: Getting Together the Rough Draft

IT'S ABOUT TIME

It's important to leave yourself enough time before the due date to be able to write at least one rough draft. (In fact, many professional writers admit to writing six or seven drafts of something until it pleases them!) If there's one thing A+ compositions probably have in common, it's that they are all products of at least one revision. To do this, and to do it well, you must arrange your time wisely. You need to be able to dash off your rough draft, then put it aside for a while. You need time to get away from it so that when you

27

are face-to-face with it again, you can look at it freshly, with the enthusiasm that you may have lost had you been locked up together for too long a time. Sometimes writing that looked bad yesterday looks much better today. Arrange your time so that pressure doesn't force you to hand in something less than your best.

STARTING IS HALF THE BATTLE

If you have trouble getting started writing, you are normal. But it is a known fact that when the first word is written, you're on your way. So, sharpen your pencils or change the typewriter ribbon, feed the dog, dry the dishes, and get going! Simply sit, with your outline in front of you, and type or scribble the first words that come into your head.

The trick is to write your first draft as fast as possible. Resist the temptation to stop and revise after every few lines or paragraphs. Don't worry at this point about details like spelling, punctuation, or even sentence structure. If, while you're writing, you can't think of a particular word, leave a blank and fill it in later. Your purpose is to get your thoughts down on paper in a fairly organized manner that will be polished up on your second (or even third) time around. (Just be sure to leave extra-wide margins and lots of space between lines so you'll have room to revise on the same paper.)

As you're writing your first draft, remember that your outline was not chiseled in stone. If you find as you go along that it needs to be rear-ranged — do it. Many writers find that once they start writing they must reorganize as the paper proceeds. But having an outline in the first place gives you a place to start and helps to save time and frustration.

SOLID FOUNDATIONS: THE BASICS OF PARAGRAPHING

Don't be nervous about writing a good compo-sition because if you can write a good paragraph, you're more than halfway there. A single para-graph is like a mini-composition. And, a good single paragraph is planned as thoroughly as a good composition. It has a single controlling idea, it uses a variety of details to develop that idea, and it ties all the ideas together into one logical group of sentences. Each group of sen-tences (the paragraph) should work together to advance the overall theme of the paper.

If paragraphs didn't exist, it wouldn't take a reader too long to get tired of looking at an entire page of writing that goes on and on without a break. You need to guide the reader along with signs of where you are going with your thinking. Paragraphs provide these signs and indicate to a reader where one idea leaves off and another begins. Obviously, good paragraphs don't just happen — they're created. Here's more on how.

Topic Sentences

The sentence which presents the topic to be

discussed within the paragraph is called the topic sentence. Every other sentence in the paragraph should be closely related to this topic sentence.

Many writers place their topic sentence at or near the beginning of the paragraph. A topic sentence near the beginning helps both you and your reader by clearly stating the main point of the paper before going on to develop it. However, in a long composition, it would be boring and monotonous to have the topic sentence at the beginning of every paragraph. So, it's a good practice to alternate the position of your topic sentence. For a change of pace, try it in the middle or at the end of the paragraph. As long as you use good supporting sentences to develop the topic sentence, feel free to move it where you think it will be most effective.

Here are some "shapes" your paragraphs might take depending on where you place the all-important topic sentence:

The Funnel Paragraph
Topic Sentence at the Beginning

Although I know there's a gimmick behind every trick, magic will never fail to amaze me. Yesterday, as my parents and I watched closely, my brother made a coin disappear. I suspect that it wasn't an ordinary coin, but when he let me look it over it appeared very real. Perhaps I'll check out a book on Houdini and learn how to make my brother disappear!

The Diamond Paragraph
Topic Sentence in the Middle

Yesterday, as
my parents and I
watched closely, my brother
made a coin disappear. I suspect
that it wasn't an ordinary coin but when
he let me look it over it appeared very real.
**Although I know there's a gimmick behind every
trick, magic will never fail to amaze me.**
Perhaps I'll check out a book on Houdini
and learn how to make my brother
disappear!

The Pyramid Paragraph
Topic Sentence at the End

Yesterday, as
my parents and I
watched closely, my
brother made a coin disappear.
I suspect that it wasn't an ordinary
coin, but when he let me look it over it
appeared very real. Perhaps I'll check out a book
on Houdini and learn how to make my brother disappear! **Although I know there's a gimmick behind every trick,
magic will never fail to amaze me.**

Developing Topic Sentences into Paragraphs

Once you've written a topic sentence you usually can't let it stand alone. What you need now is a group of sentences that will support the idea expressed in your topic sentence. Here are six main ways you can build evidence to support your topic sentence:

1. with facts
2. with examples
3. with an incident or anecdote
4. with reasons
5. with comparisons or contrasts
6. with definitions

The support sentences that you create may be any one (or a combination) of the above methods. The important thing is to fully and effectively develop the topic sentence. If you give it little or no support, your entire paragraph will be weakened.

Here's the list again. But this time each method is accompanied by an example. Study these methods and keep them in mind whenever you begin writing.

1. A paragraph may be developed with facts. Supporting your topic sentence with factual information may make what you are saying more believable. Just make certain that you are distinguishing between fact and opinion. A fact is something that can be demonstrated to be true. An opinion, no matter how expert, is not necessarily based on fact.

This year's homecoming weekend proved to be the costliest in Glenbrook High's history. The athletic department bought new uniforms for the football team at a cost of over four hundred dollars. The "Welcome Back" brunch, sponsored by the senior class, served 150 alumni for a grand total of two hundred dollars. And, the junior class, anxious to put on a dance worth remembering, spent one hundred dollars on decorations alone.

2. A paragraph may be developed with examples. Good examples can help to illustrate a topic that deals with something abstract (like beauty, truth, or freedom) because they give your reader something concrete to relate to.

Jenny is one of the nicest people I've ever met. For instance, if you're out of school just one day, Jenny is the type of friend who is first to call and find out what's wrong. She's also the kind of person to lend a helping hand, whether it's with homework, babysitting, or even washing the dishes. Another thing about Jenny is that she always has time to listen to her friends. I think her middle initial, "C," stands for "Consideration."

3. A paragraph may be developed with an incident or anecdote. Telling a brief story can be an interesting way of supporting the idea in your topic sentence. Of course, an incident or anecdote is a particular type of example. But they are examples with a story behind them. Just make sure that the story you tell is clearly related to the idea expressed in the topic sentence.

Some people have to learn the hard way that cheating is a dangerous game. A friend of mine, who put off doing a research paper until the last minute, ended up handing in his older brother's B+ paper from five years before. When the paper was returned, it was marked with a red F at the top. "An F?" Glenn said to our teacher. "But I thought it was clearly at least a B+." "It was worth a B+," the teacher explained, "when your brother, Marc, first handed it in to me five years ago."

4. A paragraph may be developed with reasons. This is a good way to develop a paragraph whose topic sentence prompts a reader to immediately ask the question, "Why?" If you're trying to get a point across or give your side of an argument, try building a paragraph with logical reasons (that may themselves be supported by facts, examples, or incidents) that explain why you think and feel the way you do.

My parents just won't let me grow up. It seems that they watch over everything I do! They refuse to let me stay out after midnight — even on weekends! And, even though I have my driver's license, I can't take the car out alone. It's wonderful to be loved, but it's frustrating to be babied.

5. A paragraph may be developed with comparisons and contrasts. Sometimes you can clarify the idea expressed in the topic sentence by comparing or contrasting it with a similar, more familiar, idea.

A blind date can turn an ordinary Saturday night into a very special evening. Of course, accepting a blind date, like buying a lottery ticket, is taking a chance. But a lot of lottery tickets are winners, and the same is true of blind dates. Just don't get too easily discouraged; give yourself time to get to know the person. Remember that he or she took a chance, too!

6. A paragraph may be developed with definitions. When you really want to make your reader understand what you mean by a particular word or phrase contained in the topic sentence, and a short definition just won't do, you may want to devote a whole paragraph to the definition. This method may involve giving many facts and examples in order to make yourself clear.

Gorging yourself with "junk" food is the first sign you're on the road to ruin. Sugary, high-carbohydrate foods are high on calories and low on nourishment. A steady diet of cake, candy, cookies, soda pop, potato chips, pretzels, and ice cream will only make you fat, moody, and run-down. In short, they'll ruin your health.

IS THAT A FACT? SUPPORTING YOUR STATEMENTS

No one has to take your word for anything. Remember that truth as you write your first draft. No matter what type of paper you're writing, if you state something as a fact, be certain to include evidence that backs up your position. Not doing so will indicate that you did little or no research and could make your teacher think it was a last minute or lazy effort on your part.

Build a solid, thorough paper. If it's a report on the energy crisis, don't throw in a statement like, "More and more homes will soon convert to solar power," and let it go at that. Unless you qualify as a known energy specialist, no one is under any obligation to accept what you've said as true. Verify such a statement with a variety of facts quoted from newspapers, magazines, or television reports, and support the statement with quotes from architects, engineers, or government energy specialists. Do whatever you can to make your statements sound strong and full of authority.

Supporting a statement with facts does not mean, however, that you're not entitled to offer your opinion anywhere in the paper. Of course you can give an opinion about something as long as you make it clear that you are expressing your own view. In book and movie reviews, and some subject reports, your teacher will expect a personal opinion. Just remember to use the personal pronoun "I" in these instances where you are clearly speaking for yourself.

THE LONG AND THE SHORT OF IT: DETERMINING PARAGRAPH LENGTH

Generally, the length of a paragraph is determined by the topic sentence and the number of details that must be included to make the idea you are trying to get across clear and effective. However, even though there is no strict rule as to paragraph length, unless you're writing a personal letter or dialogue, anything much less than one hundred words is likely to be weak. Provide as much information as you can so that your paragraphs are adequately developed. (Two exceptions to this may be your introductory and concluding paragraphs, which are more for attention and emphasis and might benefit by being shorter than the developmental paragraphs.)

Looking at this from another direction, however, if your paragraph runs over three hundred words, you may be straying from the main idea. Be aware that you run the risk of confusing and/or losing a reader if your paragraphs are too long and include ideas not closely related to the topic sentence.

GOOD CONNECTIONS: MAKING SMOOTH TRANSITIONS

To be really good, your writing must be like a chain. The sentences and paragraphs must be linked together for strength and unity. Each sentence should have a connection to the one before it and, similarly, each paragraph should be a natural extension of the previous one. Making logical connections in your writing relies on good use of transitional words and phrases.

If you work at attaining smooth transition in your writing, your reports and compositions will be more understandable. It takes practice, but both you and your reader will be happier with a paper that really "hangs" together. Following are some specific ways to help you learn to make the right connections.

Pronouns As Linking Expressions

In order to keep the thoughts moving smoothly from sentence to sentence and paragraph to paragraph, use pronouns to refer to words or ideas in the preceding sentences or paragraphs. These pronouns will carry the reader back to what has just been said. They're sort of like built-in memory devices so you can be confident that your reader is following your train of thought.

The pronouns commonly used as linking expressions are *he, she, they, this, that, these, those, them,* and *it. This, that, these,* and *those,* when used as adjectives, also work as transitional devices.

Roller skating is an old-fashioned sport that has become an overnight sensation. *It* seems to be most popular with the disco crowds. *They* have changed their dancing shoes for roller skates and can be seen rolling to their favorite tunes at all hours of the day and night. Some may think *that* sounds a little crazy, but any roller-disco person will tell you, *"It's* just good, clean fun!"

You will probably understand *this* new fad much better if you actually try skating on your own. There are plenty of roller discos that rent skates to beginners. Just be sure to wear plenty of padding in case your sense of balance isn't what *it* used to be!

Connectives

Another kind of transitional device is a word or expression that connects what has preceded with what is to follow. These types of devices are called *connectives.* Use connectives to make your writing coherent. But be careful because too many of these words within one paper will make your writing seem awkward and artificial.

Here's a list of many commonly used connectives. Note that they are grouped according to their effect on your writing. Keep this in mind when you're about to use a connective, and choose one that would best suit your purpose.

CONNECTIVES USED TO INDICATE A TIME OR SPATIAL RELATIONSHIP:

soon, next, then, later, finally, eventually, first, second, (third, etc.), now, meanwhile, in the meantime, afterward, since, nearby, above, below, beyond, in front (in back), to the right (left).

CONNECTIVES USED TO INDICATE A SEQUENCE (TO ADD ANOTHER THOUGHT):

and, in addition, also, furthermore, moreover, another, likewise, similarly, next, finally, besides, again, first of all, secondly.

CONNECTIVES USED TO INDICATE CONTRAST:

but, on the other hand, however, rather, nevertheless, otherwise, yet, still, in spite of.

CONNECTIVES USED TO INDICATE RESULTS:

therefore, hence, because, thus, consequently, as a result, for, accordingly, so.

CONNECTIVES USED TO INDICATE EXAMPLES:

for instance, an example of this, for example, take the case of, in other words.

Big cars should be banned from the roads. *First of all*, they drink enormous amounts of fuel that is fast becoming scarce. *Secondly*, they poison the air with excessive exhaust fumes. *And, in addition to* both those things, they are demanding parking space that our cities just don't have the room to provide.

In spite of all the evidence against large-size cars, however, Detroit manufacturers still turn out a good number of them each year. They say there are still many orders for such vehicles, and, until the American people stop buying them, they will continue to be produced.

Repetition of a Key Word or Phrase

Help readers bridge the gap between paragraphs by repeating a key word or phrase from one paragraph in the first sentence of the next paragraph. Not only does this practice serve to carry thoughts from one part to the next, but it also acts as a means of emphasizing an important point.

Karen was upset over her misunderstanding with Lois. But she had thought it would blow over and everything would get back to the way it used to be. She never thought that the rumors would start. At least now she knew who her *real friends* were.

One of these *real friends* was Alison. Thank goodness she was one person who didn't listen to gossip. . . !

Direct References

Another way to keep your readers on track is by using direct references. You can refer directly back to a word or an idea used in preceding sentences and paragraphs by using synonyms (for a word) and summaries (of an idea).

Paul is a terrific guy who lives next door to us. He's always ready to lend a helping hand and you can tell that he really cares about the people who live in this part of town. When he rescued one of the little kids from a burning garage, *our neighbor* proved he was brave as well as kind.

Today, this *neighborhood "Superman"* will be honored by the town. It's wonderful how *that fourteen-year-old boy* can be such an inspiration to us all.

GRAND OPENINGS: CATCHING A READER'S INTEREST

The beginning of any paper is probably the most important part that you will write. It has the huge responsibility of presenting your thesis and making your purpose clear *and* of arousing the interest of the readers so they'll want to read further. One way to look at your introductory or opening paragraph is to compare it to bait that you're going to cast into a "sea" of potential readers. Here are some ideas on how to "hook" these readers from the very beginning:

The Plunge-Right-In Opener

Plunging right into your subject is a direct and very acceptable way of catching a reader's interest. But in using this approach, avoid at all cost such awkward statements as "This essay is about . . ." or "I am going to show that. . . ." Being direct and to the point is not a license to be boring. Bore your reader in line one and she or he may not be awake to learn that the rest of the paper is a winner!

Here are two plunge-right-in openers that aren't boring:

"New York has the dubious distinction of being closer than any other major city to a nuclear power plant."
> —Nan Randall, "What if . . .?"
> *New York* magazine, April 16, 1979.

"Journalists have been dismayed recently by a series of court decisions allowing searches of their news rooms, their notebooks and their phone records."
> — David Gelman and Diane Camper,
> "Probing a Newsman's Mind,"
> *Newsweek*, April 30, 1979.

The Startling Statement Opener

A good, attention-getting opening paragraph includes a statement of fact or opinion that will intrigue or shock your reader. What you want to do is catch the reader by surprise and entice him to read further.

Here are some famous openings that may have already shocked or interested you:

"I don't think I'll ever get married."
— Judy Blume, *It's Not the End of the World.*

"I was sick — sick unto death with that long agony; and when they at length unbound me, and I was permitted to sit, I felt that my senses were leaving me."
— Edgar Allan Poe, "The Pit and the Pendulum."

The Question Opener

Asking a question at the beginning of your introductory paragraph is a good way to make it clear what your paper is all about. Your reader assumes that if she or he reads further, the question will be answered. (And, it is your responsibility to make certain it is answered!) It is also a good way to start because it forces the reader to think about the subject.

Are you familiar with these question openers?

"What can you say about a twenty-five-year-old girl who died?"
— Erich Segal, *Love Story.*

"How do we go about living a nourishing life?"
— Dr. Jerry Greenwald, *Be the Person You Were Meant to Be.*

The Story Opener

Everyone likes a good story and telling one at the beginning of a composition is an excellent way to attract your readers' attention. Just be absolutely positive that the story you tell is fairly brief and is related to the purpose of your paper. Because of an easy, informal style to storytelling, relating incidents or anecdotes can be as interesting to write as well as to read.

Here are the first few lines of some good story openers:

"The other night, a friend of mine sat down at the table and informed me that if I was going to write a column about women, I ought to deal straight off with the subject most important to women in all the world. 'What is that?' I asked. 'Beauty,' she said."
— Nora Ephron, "On Never Having Been a Prom Queen."

"One night, ten years ago, my father was complaining about his job. After 40 years of selling women's hats on the same street in Manhattan, the pay was still lousy, his boss didn't give a damn about him and nobody bought hats anymore . . ."
— Bernard Lefkowitz, "Life Without Work," *Newsweek*, May 14, 1979.

The Direct Quote Opener

Sometimes quoting someone else makes an unusual and interesting opening. The speaker may be an authority on your topic, the subject of your topic, or just someone (famous or not) who has made a pertinent comment about your topic. If you're writing a piece of fiction, it might be one of your characters who introduces the topic via a bit of dialogue. Some writers find that a "spoken" introduction adds importance or meaning.

How about these openers?

" 'Once you're successful, you can meet almost anybody in the world you want to meet,' says The Rolling Stones lead vocalist Mick Jagger."
— "Mick Jagger: On Rockin' and Rollin' and Running Around," *Celebrity* magazine,
September 1977.

" 'I had a couple of lean years,' says golfer John Mahaffey, 31. 'It takes a while to get everything back into shape.' "
— *People* magazine article on John Mahaffey, by Jim Calio, August 6, 1979.

As you can see by all of these examples, there's more than one way to catch a reader's interest. And, once you've got him on the line, don't let him get away!

Generally speaking, the length of your introduction should be directly related to the length of the entire essay. If your thesis can be supported with only three or four well-developed paragraphs, then one introductory paragraph will probably do the trick. But an essay with six or more major points (as you might have in some research papers) may require more than one paragraph to adequately introduce the topic.

One more thing about your introductory paragraph — don't include too much information. Your objective is to inform the reader just a little bit, but intrigue him a lot. Once you've hooked a reader, then you can load him up with information. But don't scare him away before you get the chance. Follow the method of newspapers the world over. They have a "lead" paragraph that includes the basics, "hooking" the reader from the start. Details can be revealed as your paper progresses.

MARVELOUS MIDDLES: KEEPING A READER'S INTEREST

Once you've created an opening that will "hook" your readers, you must get to the heart of the paper. Known as the "middle," the "body," or the "developmental paragraphs," this section is made up of what you have to say. It will be the longest part of the paper and will need careful organization. Here's where knowing how to develop a paragraph comes in handy!

A marvelous middle (and even the not-so-marvelous one) consists of a group of paragraphs (usually three to five paragraphs in an "average" length composition), with a structure similar to that of a single paragraph. Just as the topic sentence states the main idea of a single paragraph, your introduction states the main idea of your paper. And, similarly, as the main points of a paragraph are developed according to facts, examples, incidents, reasons, comparison and contrasts, and definitions, the main points of an entire paper are developed in the same ways. (Review the details of these methods of development in the first part of this chapter on page 32.)

It's a good idea to refer to your outline when concentrating on the middle of your paper. Hopefully you will have arranged the details according to a tentative plan. But if you haven't yet thought of a logical order for the details of your paper (or have changed your mind about what you'll include) reread the section, "Suitable Arrangements," in Chapter 1, page 21.

EXCEPTIONAL ENDINGS: CONCLUDING ON AN INTERESTING NOTE

A good piece of writing, like a good meal, leaves a person with a satisfying feeling. So, create your endings as carefully as you would a delectable dessert.

A whole paragraph of summary or conclusion may not be necessary. In a short paper, one or two concluding sentences are usually enough. But whatever the length, an ending should somehow remind the reader what it is you have said. It should summarize or reemphasize the major points of the composition or it may make a prediction about the future of the subject. And, since it's your last chance to get a point across, it may include a personal thought or opinion (just be sure you make it clear that it is an opinion and not a fact) or relevant quote.

A good ending will give the reader a sense of completion. But in creating one, stay away from endings with such phrasing as "And so I have shown that . . ." or "Now for my conclusion . . ." or "I hope you now realize that. . . ." A conclusion doesn't have to be labeled as such! If it's a good wrap-up of what was said, your readers will know what it is. Don't spoil your last contact with them by boring or insulting them. Keep it interesting to the end! They might even thank you for it.

Here are some exceptional endings that might prove interesting and inspirational:

"When all of this was done, a republic eventually came to pass but the sorrows, and the troubles have never left that tragic, lovely land. For you see, in Ireland there is no future, only the past happening over and over."

— Leon Uris, *Trinity*.

"And what I have called *The Amityville Horror* remains one of those dark mysteries that challenges our conventional accounting of what this world contains."

— Jay Anson, *The Amityville Horror*.

" 'We came into this world to work together, but we can't be Bee Gees forever.' Why stop now? Says Robin, 'We want to go out on top.' "

— Jim Jerome, "Hanging Out with the Bee Gees," *People* magazine, August 6, 1979.

Chapter 3

MATTERS OF STYLE: IMPROVING THE *WAY* YOU WRITE

Your style is the *way* you write as opposed to what you write about (the contents or message of your paper). Imagine two articles on the same subject. One writer produced an interesting paper while the other writer's paper was quite dull. How could something like that happen? The difference is probably in the *style* of their writing.

While there are no rights and wrongs regarding personal style, there are certain qualities that an interesting style does exhibit. By studying these qualities and learning to incorporate them into your own writing, you can turn out more interesting A+ papers in no time.

TONE TACTICS

In speech, hearing the tone of a person's voice helps you to understand fully the meaning of his or her words. For example, if a friend comes up to you after class and says, "I barely passed the English test," you can tell just by the tone of his voice (and perhaps the look on his face) whether he is surprised, happy, disappointed, or angered. Did he study hard and is disappointed at not getting an A? Is he surprised at doing so "well," considering he never cracked a book? Or is he happy because he crammed the last minute and just wanted a passing grade? Obviously, the words themselves convey only part of the meaning. It's the *tone* that gives words "personality" and emphasis, letting you know how a speaker feels.

Tone also exists in writing — it's the *sound* your writing makes. But, in this case, since the words are read and not heard, an author must communicate tone through word choice and sentence structure. Generally, there are two tones: the *objective* or impersonal (informative) tone; and the *subjective* or personal (emotional) tone.

An objective tone conveys information without showing anything about the writer's personal feeling or personality. It is most appropriate when you are writing expository essays, news articles, lab reports, and research papers.

The subjective personal tone also informs readers but mainly it communicates a writer's feeling or attitude about the subject. A subjective tone should be used when writing any kind of review, autobiography, or personal letters, as well as most persuasive and narrative essays.

Here are three things that you should consider before beginning to write any paper. Keeping them in mind will help you to create a tone that will produce the effect you want.

1. Think of your attitute toward your topic. What is your topic? How do you *feel* about this topic? What is your thesis? Is it something with which you agree or disagree? Are you sympathetic or detached? Are you amused or outraged? Be aware of your attitude so you can control whether or not it comes across in your writing. Some reports call for a formal, impersonal, detached manner, while some essays and book reports almost require that your attitude be clear to readers. Take a stand before you start.

2. Think of your purpose. What do you want to accomplish by writing this paper? Is it to present factual information? Is it to entertain? Is it to persuade readers, win them over to a cause you believe in? Is it to give your opinion of something? Is it to impress your teacher and get an A?

3. Think of your audience. Keep in mind who might be reading your paper. Your teacher? Your classmates? A group of nuclear scientists? A class of third graders? Once you've identified who you will be writing for, it is your responsibility to write in terms they will understand. This does not mean that you should change the facts or alter your beliefs in order to impress or interest your readers, but it does mean that you should use language that these particular readers will both understand and appreciate. After all, you don't *speak* to friends, parents, little children, teachers, doctors, or strangers with the same words or in the same voice. You'll find that the same practice holds true in writing.

When you are aware of your attitude, purpose, and audience, the right tone will almost occur automatically. But, most importantly, once you decide on a tone, be consistent. Abrupt changes can confuse a reader. If you start out in a subjective tone, stay in the subjective tone. There's nothing wrong with giving information along with your personal feelings as long as you don't suddenly switch to the more objective, impersonal voice. Give your paper one "personality" and be proud of it.

ON THE LEVEL: FORMAL, INFORMAL, AND COLLOQUIAL LANGUAGE

Most people choose to wear clothes that fit their mood as well as the occasion. Writers choose words for the same reasons. So, just as you might dress one way for a football game and another way for the junior prom, you might "dress" your writing one way for a book report and another way for a term paper.

The tone, or "personality," you want your paper to project will be established by the type of words and sentence structure you choose to use. Generally, your writing will fall into one of three categories or levels of English — Formal, Informal, or Colloquial (Non-Standard). Each level has its particular uses although there is crossover in some cases.

The chart below summarizes the three basic levels of language. Use it as a guide and *not* as a rulebook. Notice that most of your writing is, and should be, on an informal level. Some term papers may call for the technical language of a formal style and you might use slang in the dialogue of an informal, narrative essay. The important thing is always to use the language appropriate to the purpose of your composition.

LEVEL	CHARACTERISTICS	USES
FORMAL	Specialized or difficult vocabulary, relatively long sentences, few contractions, no slang, proper usage and punctuation, objective or serious tone.	Government and legal documents, medical reports, research papers, some textbooks, essays and articles for a *specialized* audience, serious speeches and lectures, some business letters and reports.
INFORMAL	Sentences of varying lengths, commonly used vocabulary (including idioms, slang, and contractions *where appropriate*), popular usage, personal *or* objective tone.	Newspapers, magazines, most textbooks, short school reports and essays, letters to friends and family, some business letters, political speeches.
COLLOQUIAL (Non-Standard)	Short, very simple sentences, grammatical errors, much slang, misspellings, limited vocabulary, localisms.	Dialogue intended to represent local dialects in books, plays, comics, movies, radio, and television.

SCINTILLATING SENTENCE STRUCTURES: HOW TO VARY YOUR SENTENCES

Your writing style will be more effective if you vary the length and structure of your sentences. Sentences having the same pattern and the same rhythm throughout your paper will produce a monotonous, choppy effect that could make your composition tiresome and boring to read.

If your paper is loaded with short sentences all starting with the subject, it's time for a change. Here are some suggestions on how to go from simple to compound and complex sentences and from the normal order of subject — predicate — complement, to other, more interesting arrangements.

1. Place the direct object of a verb before the subject.

Tears and anger I had expected, but total silence surprised me.

2. Begin your sentence with an adjective or with an adverb.

Wrinkled and leathery, the man's face was clearly a sign of old age.

Quietly entering the room, I took a seat in the back.

3. Open a sentence with a prepositional or a participial phrase.

Through the open window I could see the family eating their dinner.

Having known him all my life, I was convinced he was innocent.

4. For special effect, start a sentence with a coordinating conjunction, such as *and, or, nor* **or** *but.*

And, believe it or not, she lied!

But let me explain.

5. Try separating the subject and predicate by words or phrases.

The movie, *frightening and fast-paced,* was really terrific.

6. Occasionally, write a sentence that is a question or exclamation.

Isn't it time we helped the elderly in our neighborhood?

Volunteer, today!

7. Make a series of short, simple sentences into a longer, complex sentence.

Not this: Eric Lane is captain of North's football team. He showed up at Saturday's carnival alone. He and his girlfriend broke up.

But this: Eric Lane, captain of North's football team, showed up at Saturday's carnival alone because he and his girlfriend broke up.

8. Avoid long, "stringy" sentences that are put together by the overuse of the words *and* **and** *so.*

Use subordination of ideas (add clauses and/or

phrases) to replace and *and* so:

Not this: The temperature outside continues to fall *and* people's fear and anxiety grow, *and* this makes them nervous about not having enough fuel to heat their homes.

But this: As the temperature outside continues to fall, people's fear and anxiety grow, making them nervous about not having enough fuel to heat their homes.

Divide one sentence into two:

Not this: Ryan is a baseball fan *and so* he goes to every home game *and* he buys the best seats in the stadium *so* he can see better *and* maybe catch a foul ball.

But this: Being a baseball fan, Ryan goes to every home game. Since he buys the best seats in the stadium, he not only sees better, but is in a good position to catch a foul ball.

TAKE ACTION: USING ACTIVE VERBS

In writing, the difference between the active voice and the passive voice makes all the difference in the world. An active voice verb makes a sentence more direct and lively. A passive voice verb, however, is less forceful, and using a lot of them in one paper can produce awkward, less effective sentences.

The **active voice** of a verb shows who or what

59

is doing something — as in *Peter hit Matt* or *The wind pushed me down*. The **passive voice** shows who or what is being acted on — as in *Matt was hit by Peter* or *I was pushed by the wind*. As you can see from the examples, the active voice sentences are more concise and convey a more concrete picture than the sentences with passive verbs.

Although both the active voice and the passive voice are grammatically correct, active verbs are usually preferred. About the only instance a passive verb would be preferred would be when you want to emphasize the object of the sentence — by making it the subject. For instance, instead of *I will order the cake next week,* if you want to emphasize the *cake,* switch the sentence to read: *The cake will be ordered next week.*

TELL IT LIKE IT IS: THE ART OF BEING SPECIFIC

When you learn the "art" of using words to paint clear pictures of what you are saying, you'll be less likely to leave your reader pondering over blurred meanings. Words have color and texture just as paints do. And, to obtain the effect you want, you must choose the words as carefully as an artist would choose his color of paint.

For an A+ composition, use top-quality words to express your ideas. (But don't make the mistake of thinking that the best word is the one with more than seven syllables that fewer than five classmates know how to pronounce!) Memorize this rule: The best word to use is always the one that conveys the *exact* meaning you intend. The reader should never have to scratch his head, wondering what you are trying to say. Any abstract words (i.e., something which *cannot* be touched or seen: beauty, love, freedom, happiness) must translate into clear, exact meanings. Any concrete words (something that *can* be touched or seen: car, house, flower, food) must be made as specific as possible.

All words create mental images in a reader's mind, but these images are not necessarily the same in every reader. When you see the word "house," what do *you* think of? Your own house? Your best friend's house? A mansion? A shack? It all depends on your frame of reference. But a good writer can narrow down a reader's mental image of an abstract or non-specific word by being as descriptive as possible. Burt's house. A treehouse. The White House. An estate. A farmhouse. And, the more you narrow something down, the more concrete it becomes. Burt's giant, colonial house. A rickety, old treehouse, etc. The list of houses is endless, so if you have a particular one in mind, say so. If your words are too abstract, a reader will visualize what *he* wants to and may miss your point entirely.

"Food" is not at all specific; "hamburger, french fries, and a milk shake" are more specific. "Vehicle" is not at all specific; "car, bus, and motorcycle" are more specific. "Dog" is not at all specific; "French poodle, German shepherd, and fox terrier" are more specific. Too many abstract or non-specific concrete words in a paper will make your writing vague and underdeveloped. A reader needs enough specific concrete words to make the abstract clearer and more familiar.

Liven up your style and be as concrete as possible. Here are three good ways to do just that:

1. Illustrate abstract and non-specific concrete words with carefully chosen adjectives and adverbs.
(Note the words "carefully chosen." A sentence with seven mediocre adjectives and/or adverbs won't be as effective as a sentence with one or two *well-chosen* ones.)

Instead of: The guests were impressed by the food.

How about? The guests were impressed by an appetizing array of hot and cold food, elegantly served in the traditional Japanese style.

2. Illustrate abstract and non-specific concrete words with concrete examples.

Instead of: There were many delicious foods to eat at the picnic.

How about? There were platters of cheese and crackers; a huge buffet table covered with chicken, potato salad, cole slaw, and corn; wooden bowls overflowing with fruit; and mouth-watering strawberry shortcakes smothered with whipped cream.

3. Illustrate abstract and non-specific concrete words with similes and metaphors. *(Reminder: A* simile *is a direct comparison using the* *words "like" or "as." A* metaphor *is an implied comparison — it does not use "like" or "as.")*

Instead of: The guests ate a lot of food.
How about? The guests ate like vultures.

Instead of: The table had a lot of food on it.
How about? The table was a mountain of
chicken and potato salad.

Help your readers to see, hear, feel, taste, and touch your words. Be specific. Be concrete. You'll be understood.

SHADES OF MEANING: RECOGNIZING THE CONNOTATIONS OF WORDS

Every word is made up of two parts, its *denotative* and its *connotative* meaning. The strict dictionary definition or basic meaning of a word is its *denotation*. For example, the word "tall" denotes "high in stature." Any pleasant or unpleasant associations, feelings, or suggested meanings of a word that go beyond its basic, denotative meaning are called *connotations*. Connotations of a word may be favorable or unfavorable depending upon each reader's specific personal reaction. Therefore, the word "tall" might connote "large" to one person, "graceful" to another, and "gawky" to a third.

Words that tend to have neither a favorable

nor an unfavorable connotation for most people are called *neutral words*. They may convey your meaning adequately, but do nothing toward giving the reader any specifics. Words such as street, liquid, restaurant, boat, drink, said, etc., are all examples of neutral words. These kinds of words will rely on surrounding words to give them more strength and meaning.

As a writer you can, of course, choose to write with only neutral words. But think how colorless and boring such writing would be! Instead, train yourself to be aware of the connotations of various words. When you want to express feelings that are favorable or unfavorable, try to select words that will have the right connotations for your purpose.

The examples below illustrate the range of positive and negative connotative meanings. Even though all three sentences in each set may share the same *basic* meaning, notice how the different connotations really contribute to the overall meaning.

Neutral: Brian *saves his money*.
Favorable: Daniel *is thrifty*.
Unfavorable: Andy *is cheap*.

Neutral: Gail is *short*.
Favorable: Lisa is *petite*.
Unfavorable: Alana is *shrimpy*.

Neutral: I rode in the *car*.
Favorable: Esther rode in the *limousine*.
Unfavorable: Charles rode in the *clunker*.

Neutral: Joyce ate in a *restaurant*.
Favorable: Richard ate in a *hotel dining room*.
Unfavorable: Steve ate in a *dive*.

Remember that the words you choose will influence your readers. Some words are "loaded" with connotation and must be used with care. Stuck in the wrong place they can change the whole tone and thus the whole meaning of your paper. After all, a *shrimpy* guy who drives a *clunker* and eats in a *dive* isn't necessarily *cheap*. Maybe he's just *thrifty*!

NOBODY SPEAKS "JARGONESE": AVOIDING CONFUSING WORDS

Most likely, your paper will not be put on a scale and assigned a grade according to its weight. So why load it down with a whole troop of meaningless words?

Jargon, from the French word meaning "babble" or "chatter," is the name given to language that uses big, vague, confusing words. A common characteristic of jargon is that it takes fifty words to say what could be said in ten. And, although nobody speaks "jargonese," millions are quick to put it into their writing.

Jargon is:
> I regret to inform you that due to the fact you have canceled yet another date I must conclude our relationship.

When what the writer really means is:
> Because you broke another date, we're through!

A paper filled with jargon may look impressive at first glance, but begin to read it and it won't really make sense. Pretentious and confusing, this kind of writing does nothing more than take up space and irritate a reader because he can't figure out what is being said. If a reader isn't sure about what a writer is trying to say, he or she can't reasonably judge the ideas and might take the easy way out by putting the paper aside and ignoring it. (Or, in a teacher's case, by giving it a poor grade.)

Why would a person purposely use jargon? Perhaps he or she is not clear on what to present in the paper. Inflated words tend to cover up poorly developed thoughts. But it's a thin disguise and sooner or later a reader will figure it out (probably sooner than later). If you're unsure of what to say in a paper or how to say it, take some time to think your ideas through before beginning to write. In the end, you'll save time, effort, and possible embarrassment. If you're at all confused about where you're going, how can you possibly lead anyone else there?

Another reason that some people use jargon is that they think it sounds impressive. But not many people are impressed by something that they don't understand. They just get frustrated and confused. Don't try to show off with jargon. It won't work. Be brief . . . and be yourself. Write with words that don't need a translation.

Here are two famous proverbs written in "jargonese." Can you translate them into plain English?

A. It is advisable under most circumstances to restrain any impulses to numerically order one's poultry before the completion of incubation.

B. In my opinion it would be unwise under the circumstances for those who inhabit glass dwellings to throw any geological specimens.

If it took you a while to figure out that A is, *Don't count your chickens before they're hatched* and B is, *People who live in glass houses shouldn't throw stones*, then think how long it would take you to understand an entire paper written in this language! Do yourself and your readers a favor and stick to plain talking.

SHORTCUTS: A GUIDE TO PLAIN TALKING

Learn to minimize jargon in your papers by remembering that it's word quality and not quantity that counts in writing. Eliminate phrases that just take up room in a sentence and replace them with simple, more direct words. Here are some space-saving suggestions:

INSTEAD OF	USE
along the lines of	*like*
by means of	*with, by*
despite the fact that	*though*
for the reason that	*since*
in the amount of	*for*
in the event that	*if*
in view of the fact that	*because*
it's my opinion that	*I think, I believe*
make an attempt to	*try to*
on the basis of	*by, from, etc.*
subsequent to	*after, following*
with respect (regard) to	*about*

Unless you're writing a formal research or term paper, avoid purely technical terms. *Don't use a word unless you know its exact meaning.* Of course it helps to use a thesaurus, but don't use it to write your whole paper and replace simple, right-to-the-point words with what you think are their more impressive equivalents. Why say "resides" when "lives" is so much clearer? Why bother with "deem" when "think" is available? And, why would you want to "ascertain" something when "learn" is so much easier? Get the idea? Don't go out of your way to try to sound impressive and be something you're not. Get the point across with words that work fast.

One last note: Beware of meaningless, repetitious words within a phrase. Do you really need the word "down" in the sentence: "He fell *down* from the tree"? (Very few, if any, people ever fall *up*.) What about the "out" in "Erase *out* all errors"? It's unnecessary! And why use the phrase "each and every" when the word "each" *or* the word "every" works very well alone. There's no prize for wordiness, so trim all phrases wherever possible.

AVOID CLICHÉS — LIKE THE PLAGUE!

A cliché (pronounced klē sha') is a trite expression that has been used so often by so many people that it has lost the freshness and originality it once had. Certainly the first person to have used the phrase "busy as a bee" must have been thought of as pretty clever. But after years and years of seeing "busy as a bee" in print and hearing it used in conversation, it is a dull, dull, dull addition to any piece of writing. A paper filled with a bunch of clichés may give your reader the impression that you are lazy and lack originality. Learn to use simple, straightforward language instead of worn-out phrases. Make your writing reflect how thoughtful and original you can be.

Since clichés come to mind so easily, you have to consciously watch out for them so they don't creep into your sentences. *Think* while you are writing and don't always opt for the easy way out. Be creative. Substitute new words for the old standbys.

Look over the following list of worn-out clichés. Use your imagination and revise each one of them. If you're ever tempted to use one of these tired, overused expressions, turn immediately to your original revisions.

CLICHÉ	REVISION
After all is said and done	
Beyond a shadow of a doubt	
Break the ice	
Busy as a bee	
Cool as a cucumber	
Crystal clear	
Easier said than done	
Green with envy	
Heart of gold	
Last but not least	
To make a long story short	
Time flies	
White as a sheet	

BE CONSISTENT

Green traffic lights always mean "go." But what would happen if they meant "go" in your town and "stop" in the next? No doubt it would be dangerously confusing and probably cause a lot of accidents. Many drivers, stunned by the unexpected change, would become angry and frustrated. They might even give up driving! You see, a certain amount of consistency in everyday life is not boring, it's necessary. Consistency helps people feel secure when they're driving a car and, similarly, it helps them feel secure when they're reading.

How can consistency make readers feel secure? It keeps them from getting frustrated by letting them know what to expect. It lets them safely assume that some things in your paper will remain the same to the end. Following are some hints on how you can go about making your paper more consistent.

When you use names, abbreviations, initials, and numbers, make sure that you handle them the same way all through your paper. This means that you shouldn't use the full name Patricia on one page, and then, with no prior explanation, start using the nickname "Pat" on another. (It gets even more confusing if the nicknames are not just shortened versions of the originals, like switching from Richard to "Dick" or from Diane to "DeeDee.") You also can't refer to Dr. L. B. Hart on page one, and end your paper quoting him as "Leonard Hart." *You* might know that you are referring to the same person, but a reader may not make the connection.

Regarding abbreviations, a good rule to remember is not to use them except in certain instances where they are customary and therefore quite acceptable. (Acceptable abbreviations include: Mr., Mrs., Ms., Dr., Rev., St., A.D., B.C., A.M., P.M., i.e., e.g., etc.) In all other instances it is safest to spell everything out as it leaves little room for misunderstanding. If you stick to this rule, your paper shouldn't alternate between "California" and "CA" or between "France" and "FR." Don't test your reader's spelling ability. Spell it out for him.

Acronyms (words formed from the initial letter[s] of each of the successive parts [or major parts] of a longer term) are becoming more and more popular in the media. It's hard to pick up a newspaper without seeing such "words" as UNICEF, SALT, OPEC, and NASA. In addition to the acronyms there are the organizations that go by their initials even if they don't spell some sort of a pronounceable word. So we're surrounded by things like FDA, NBA, and CIA. Now if you have a terrific memory, coming upon these letters will never pose a problem. But if you are in the majority of those with not-so-great memories, you'd like a gentle reminder of what the letters stand for.

Don't ever assume that your readers have terrific memories. Make it a practice to write the name of the organization out in full when it's first mentioned in your paper. Place the acronym or initials in parentheses following the full word(s). Give your reader a chance to become familiar with the term and then later in the paper you can begin using the initials.

Consistency is the rule when it comes to your use of numbers, too. Spell out a number if it may be done in one or two words. All others should appear as numerals. For example, *1,300,275, $433.55,* and *1980* should appear as numerals, but *five, fifty cents,* and *sixty-one* should appear in words. (Of course, this does not apply to mathematical or scientific writing where most numbers are written as numerals and not spelled out.) And, never write a sentence that mixes both formats like, "Jason bought his Levis for $22.00 while I only paid fourteen dollars for mine."

ARE YOU GAME? PAINLESS VOCABULARY-BUILDING IDEAS

Believe it or not, a friendly game of *Boggle* or a heated contest on the *Scrabble* board can improve your writing style. Don't laugh at this notion, read on.

One of the biggest problems in writing any paper (after getting started, that is) is thinking of the right word at the right time. For some people word choice becomes such a slow, tedious process that their index fingers start to ache from turning so many pages in a dictionary or a thesaurus.

You can avoid some of the head, finger, and

stomach aches that writing is known to bring about if you learn to *consciously* build up your vocabulary. Searching for one specific word is so much easier if your supply of good words exceeds the demand. But keep in mind that words are not just in dictionaries — they're everywhere! Discover them in newspapers, magazines, books, pamphlets, billboards, labels, bumper stickers, boxtops, and, as mentioned above — games!

Games are a valuable means of building your vocabulary. And they're fun, too! *Scrabble, Word Power, Boggle, Words Worth, Spill 'n Spell, Probe,* and *Word Master Mind* are only some of the numerous vocabulary games out on the market today. All of them are good training for thinking of the right word at the right time — and fast. Start saving your allowance to chip in with family or friends to buy one or two of these interesting games. Prove to yourself (and others) that vocabulary-building can be a relaxing and entertaining experience.

If you make a real attempt to learn at least one new word a day, you'll be pleasantly surprised at the improvement in your writing. All it takes is effort. Now where have you heard that before?

Chapter 4

FINAL TOUCHES: EDITING, REWRITING, AND POLISHING

Congratulations! You've just written the first draft of your composition. Now you're all through, right? Wrong. Good, effective writing always involves rewriting no matter how terrific your outline is, no matter how many hours you've already spent working, no matter how smart you are, and no matter how neat your handwriting (or typing) is. *One draft just isn't enough.* Even the most professional writers have to edit, rewrite, and polish their work many times before they're satisfied with it. In fact, that's why they're known as professionals. They're thorough revisers and are rarely satisfied with a first (and sometimes even a second) draft. So, if the pros can benefit from rewriting, so can you. (The reproduction on page 77 shows page one of Sinclair Lewis's manuscript for his novel, *Babbitt*. Notice all the revisions!)

Editing and rewriting is your opportunity to iron out any of the "wrinkles" in your first draft. Of course there will be parts you don't feel need any changing, but it pays to be honest with yourself if you want to hand in the best possible paper. Would another word be better than the one you have? Are some of the sentences awkward and monotonous? Does a particular paragraph belong somewhere else in the piece? The better able you are to constructively criticize your own writing, the better the final product will be and, ultimately, the better your grade.

When you sit down to rewrite your paper, start by reading it aloud. This helps let you see your writing as your readers would see it. In fact, reading aloud is so helpful that you might want to do it several times as you work toward a finished piece.

The importance of revision as illustrated by Sinclair Lewis.

BABBITT

CHAPTER I

Roman small cap. — (I)

of Zenith
The towers ~~of a new city~~ aspired above the morning mist; austere
towers of steel, and cement, and ~~silvery~~ limestone, sturdy as cliffs and
delicate ~~as birch-trees. They were the promise of strange futures in
this American city called Zenith.~~

The mist ~~blandly covered the hundred and~~ fretted ~~buildings of~~
earlier generations: the Post Office with its shingle-tortured man-
sard, ~~and arches that supported nothing, houses of minarets and~~
~~steambly adorned lightning rods,~~ factories with stingy and sooted
windows, ~~dreadful~~ wooden tenements colored like mud.
~~stills made up most of the city, but the good~~ clean towers were
thrusting them from the business center, and on the farther hills were
~~shining~~ new houses; homes — they seemed — for laughter and tran-
quility.

Over a cement bridge ~~like carven ivory~~ slipped a limousine
~~of long sleek~~ ~~and noiseless engine.~~ The four people in evening
clothes were returning from an all-night rehearsal of a ~~Russian~~ Little Theater play — an artistic adventure ~~considerably~~ illuminated by
champagne. —

TRICKS OF THE TRADE

Careful editing and rewriting can be a slow and exacting process. So, here are some hints to help you get through it with a minimum of confusion:

1. Use a red pencil to edit. (Or any color that stands out from the color you used for the rough draft.)

2. If you discover you need to rearrange whole paragraphs (or add new ones), use a scissors to cut up the first draft and paste it back together in the order you want it. (Don't waste valuable time copying over parts you are satisfied with. Move things around and see your paper in its final new order before writing up the copy you'll hand in to your teacher.)

3. To rearrange sentences, simply draw a circle around those to be shifted and, using an arrow, show where they should be placed. If many sentences within a paragraph have to be rearranged, the circles and arrows might get too messy and confusing. In this case, *number* the sentences in the new order you want. Just make sure that when copying over the final draft you put these sentences in their new arrangement.

4. Use special proofreader's marks wherever possible. They'll save you time and make your second draft readable enough to be easily copied over into a final paper. Following is a list of the most common proofreader's marks and their meanings.

☰	(capital letter)	These three lines under a letter indicate that the letter should be capitalized.
/	(lower case or split letters or words)	This mark placed *through* a letter indicates that the letter should be lower case. Placed *between* two letters it indicates that two words should be formed.
∧	(caret insert)	This mark indicates that a word, phrase, or punctuation mark is being added.
℘	(deletion line)	This mark shows that a word, phrase, or punctuation mark is being taken out.
∾	(letter or word reversal)	This mark shows that two letters or two words should be reversed.
⊂	(connect)	This mark shows that two letters or two words should be joined together.
¶	(paragraph mark)	This mark indicates the need to indent for a new paragraph.
⊙	(period)	This indicates that a period should be added.

79

Here's an example of proofreader's marks at work:

¶ Lucy r̲. Williams⌃a student at Ridgefaild High school, won the local spelling bee and will compete in the state finals on Saturday night at the Ridge fjeld Holiday Inn. It will mean alot to Lucy if her friends are there to cheer her⌃to ⱽictory. The ¢ontest starts at 8 p.m. and admission is free⊙

YOU BE THE JUDGE: COMPOSITION CHECKLISTS

Presented below are two checklists that will help you smooth out your rough draft. When answering each question, try to be as honest as possible about your work. If in doubt about whether you should check "Yes" or "No," you might want to ask a friend to read your paper and give you *constructive* editorial comments.

1. After reading over your paper *once*, check off the items listed under "Organization and Style." *Anytime you check a "No" box, refer to the page number listed in parentheses to help you out.*

2. Reread your paper a *second* time checking for errors that relate to the "Grammar and Mechanics" section. *If you check a "No" box in this section, refer to your own grammar text or dictionary or to one of the lists at the end of this book (Spelling Demons, page 84; Punctuation Pointers, page 87).*

Organization and Style Checklist

1. My paper focuses on one specific topic. (page 13) Yes ☐ No ☐
2. I made my purpose clear from the very beginning. (page 14) Yes ☐ No ☐
3. Each paragraph presents one main idea related to the central topic. (page 19) Yes ☐ No ☐
4. The paragraphs are arranged in a logical order. (page 21) Yes ☐ No ☐
5. Each paragraph has a topic sentence (page 29) that is fully and effectively developed. (page 32) Yes ☐ No ☐
6. I have used transitions to link sentences and paragraphs. (page 38) Yes ☐ No ☐
7. I have written an attention-getting first paragraph. (page 42) Yes ☐ No ☐
8. I have written a clear conclusion. (page 48) Yes ☐ No ☐

81

9. I have used an appropriate tone. (pages 52 – 56)   Yes ☐   No ☐
10. I have varied the sentence patterns. (page 57)   Yes ☐   No ☐
11. I have used active verbs wherever possible. (page 59)   Yes ☐   No ☐
12. I have used specific, concrete words. (page 60)   Yes ☐   No ☐
13. I have said *exactly* what I mean. (page 63)   Yes ☐   No ☐
14. I have avoided jargon and tired clichés. (page 65-70)   Yes ☐   No ☐
15. My title reflects the point of my paper. (page 24)   Yes ☐   No ☐

Grammar and Mechanics Checklist

1. I have indented all paragraphs.   Yes ☐   No ☐
2. I have used only complete sentences.   Yes ☐   No ☐
3. All verbs are in the same tense throughout the paper.   Yes ☐   No ☐
4. Each sentence begins with a capital letter.   Yes ☐   No ☐
5. Each sentence ends with the proper punctuation mark. (page 87)   Yes ☐   No ☐
6. Every word is spelled correctly (see page 84 or a standard dictionary).   Yes ☐   No ☐

LAST-MINUTE MECHANICS

Most teachers will tell you how they want you to set up a paper for their particular class. But, if ever in doubt, here are some fairly universal guidelines for preparing the final copy:

1. When writing a paper by hand, use lined paper (of average spacing), 8½" x 11". Use blue or black ink, and *write neatly*.

2. If you type your paper, use 8½" x 11" white typing paper. Indent five spaces to begin new paragraphs, double space between lines of copy, and leave a 1½" margin on the left side of your paper, and a 1" margin on the right side.

3. Make certain that your name is on *all* pages of the final draft. (Preferably in the top right-hand corner.)

4. Do not number the first page of your paper (the title tells readers it's page one), but do number all subsequent pages. (Always use the numeral to indicate the page number, not the word.) Put the number beneath your name on each page.

5. Center your title at the top of your first page.

6. Proofread your final paper carefully. Don't be afraid to make changes with a pen if you notice mistakes. As long as your corrections are neatly made, your teacher probably won't consider it messy. Use common sense, though: If *you* can't read something, don't expect your teacher will be able to either.

SPELLING DEMONS

Certain words seem to stump even the best spellers over and over. One way to get over these trouble spots is to keep a record of words that repeatedly give you problems, putting special effort into memorizing them.

Fifty of the most commonly misspelled words are printed below. The next fifty lines are to be filled in by you. Record any words not already listed that tend to give you trouble (look up their correct spelling before writing them down). If it would be helpful to you, add a short definition following each word. Keep this personalized dictionary handy whenever you write and edit your compositions.

1. accommodation
2. adequate
3. a lot
4. athlete
5. bracelet
6. business
7. calendar
8. cemetery
9. competition
10. congratulations
11. definitely
12. embarrassment
13. exaggerate
14. familiarize
15. February
16. government
17. grammar
18. hospital
19. immediately
20. irresistible
21. leisurely
22. mediocre
23. mosquito
24. naive
25. occasion
26. occurrence
27. outrageous
28. pamphlet
29. pastime
30. permanent
31. pneumonia
32. privilege
33. procedure
34. professor
35. receive
36. recognize

37. recommend 42. similar 47. vacuum
38. rehearsal 43. souvenir 48. villain
39. restaurant 44. temperature 49. Wednesday
40. separate 45. truly 50. yacht
41. sergeant 46. twelfth

51. _____
52. _____
53. _____
54. _____
55. _____
56. _____
57. _____
58. _____
59. _____
60. _____
61. _____
62. _____
63. _____
64. _____
65. _____
66. _____
67. _____
68. _____

69. _____

70. _____

71. _____

72. _____

73. _____

74. _____

75. _____

76. _____

77. _____

78. _____

79. _____

80. _____

81. _____

82. _____

83. _____

84. _____

85. _____

86. _____

87. _____

88. _____

89. _____

90. _____

91. _____

92. _____

93. _____

94. _____

95. _____

96. _____

97. _____

98. _____

99. _____

100. _____

PUNCTUATION POINTERS

THE PERIOD (.)

1. Use a period after most declarative and imperative sentences.

> *Beatrice ate dinner at my house.* (Declarative)
> *Please quit asking me my name.* (Imperative)

2. Use a period after an indirect question or after a polite request.

> *Bill asked Cindy why she was late.* (Indirect question)
> *Will you please lend me your sweater.* (Polite request)

3. Use a period after standard abbreviations.

> *Ms., Mr., U.S.A., M.D., Jan., etc.*

THE QUESTION MARK (?)

1. Use a question mark at the end of a direct question.

Is Ellen home?

2. Use a question mark after each part of a sentence containing multiple questions.

Are you going to visit London? Rome? Athens?

THE COMMA (,)

Since there are dozens of possible ways to use the comma, only the most important will be listed here. A comma's main purpose is to indicate natural pauses and breaks among written words. If when you proofread you make it a habit to read your paper aloud, you will be able to *hear* where most of the commas should exist.

1. Use a comma to set off appositives (words that clarify or identify that which precedes or comes before them).

Alan, my oldest brother, leaves for college on Monday.

2. Use a comma to set off a direct address (words that tell to whom a remark is directed).

Pay attention, Fran, so you don't make a mistake.

3. Use a comma after *yes* or *no* and after weak exclamations like *oh, why,* and *well.*

Yes, I'm going to the party.
Oh, I didn't know you were invited.

4. Use a comma to separate a direct quotation from the rest of the sentence.

"I want to go bowling," said Bruce.

5. Use a comma after each word in a series.
   I ate a hamburger, french fries, and a Coke for lunch.

6. Use a comma to set off introductory clauses.
   Though he started out as the nicest teacher in school, Mr. Post turned out to be a grouch.

7. Use a comma before the state in an address.
   Chicago, Illinois

8. Use a comma between the day of the month and the year.
   January 30, 1950

9. Use a comma to separate degrees and titles from names.
   Amanda R. Tyler, Ph.D.
   Thomas Johnson, Jr.

10. Use a comma to set off transitional expressions such as however, moreover, nevertheless, therefore, etc.
    I can't meet you today. I will, however, meet you tomorrow.

THE COLON (:)

1. Use a colon to introduce a famous quotation.
   I finally understand Thoreau's famous statement: "If a man does not keep pace with his companions, perhaps it is because he hears a different drummer. Let him step to the music which he hears, however measured or far away."

2. Use a colon to prepare the reader for a list or a series.

The recipe calls for: sugar, butter, eggs, flour, and vanilla.

3. Use a colon to follow the salutation in a business letter.

Dear Sirs:

THE SEMICOLON (;)

1. Use a semicolon to separate two independent clauses when the conjunction has been omitted.

The beach was crowded; we left quite early.

2. Use a semicolon to separate items in a series that contains commas.

The names on the mailboxes read: Gordon Black, Jr.; Chris Gaynor, M.D.; and Rich Rodgers, D.C.

QUOTATION MARKS ("   ")

1. Use quotation marks to indicate titles of poems, essays, short stories, songs, and articles.

Did you read Poe's "The Tell-Tale Heart"?
My favorite song is "Send in the Clowns."

2. Use quotation marks to enclose a person's direct comments.

"I had a wonderful time," shouted Bess.

3. Use single quotation marks to indicate a quotation within a quotation.

"Yesterday," Connie said, "the baby said 'Mama' for the first time."

THE EXCLAMATION POINT (!)

1. Use an exclamation point for special emphasis, or to indicate emotion.

Watch out! Help! Stop it, now!

PARENTHESES ( )

1. Use parentheses to set off material not grammatically related to the rest of the sentence. The material should, however, explain more about the sentence in which it appears.

If you buy that dress (and I hope you do), be sure to wear it to the dance.

NOTE: Any punctuation mark belonging to the phrase that appears before the parenthesis is placed *outside* the second parenthesis mark (see example above). Only when a separate sentence is placed in parentheses is the final punctuation mark placed *inside* the parentheses (see example below).

This exam is worth one-half your final grade. (That's why you should try to answer every question.) All papers must be turned in by three o'clock.

2. Matter enclosed in parentheses within a sentence (even if it forms a complete sentence by itself) need not begin with a capital letter and need not end with a period. But, if it is a question or exclamation, it must end with the appropriate mark.

When I bought my car (it's an old, used one), suddenly I had a hundred new friends.
Lois told me that you're moving (are you?) and that she'll never see you again.

91

UNDERLINING (_____)

In writing longhand and in typing, one line under a word stands for *italics*.

1. Use underlining to indicate titles of novels, plays, paintings, newspapers, magazines, TV shows, and movies.

<blockquote>

<u>People</u> magazine is full of gossip.

You must read George Orwell's <u>Animal Farm</u>.

Did you get today's <u>Daily Sun</u>?

The movie <u>Jaws</u> was very scary.

</blockquote>

THE APOSTROPHE (')

1. Use the apostrophe to indicate possession. (Add an apostrophe and an "s" to most words to create the *singular* possessive.)

<blockquote>

I held Nancy's cat.

</blockquote>

2. Use the apostrophe to indicate possession of a *plural* word. (If it does not end in "s," add an apostrophe and an "s." If it does end in "s," just add an apostrophe.)

<blockquote>

The dogs' food might spoil.

The children's teacher is brilliant.

</blockquote>

3. Use an apostrophe to indicate the plural of numbers, letters, words, and symbols.

<blockquote>

Tony got all A's.

How many 3's are in your address?

</blockquote>

4. Use an apostrophe to show where letters have been omitted in a contraction.

<blockquote>

Ruth doesn't like pizza.

I can't read your writing.

</blockquote>

MANY HAPPY RETURNS: UNDERSTANDING YOUR TEACHER'S COMMENTS

When you get back a paper don't look only at the grade. If your teacher has made comments *read them over carefully* and use them to guide you in writing future papers. (It pays to hang on to old compositions at least for one semester or else to keep some sort of record of your strengths and weaknesses. This way you can watch your progress from assignment to assignment. For more on this, see page 114.) Only when you understand *why* you got the grade you did — whether an A, B, C, or lower — will you be able to learn how to either stay on top or rise to the top.

Frequently, because of the volume of papers they correct, many teachers use a type of shorthand or code to let you know what grammatical or mechanical errors you've made in your composition. What follows is a set of commonly accepted and useful symbols. (If your teacher uses any symbols that aren't listed here, jot down his or her originals in the blank spaces provided.) If you understand what these symbols really mean, you'll learn a lot more from your mistakes the next time around.

SYMBOL	EXPLANATION
awk	awkwardly expressed sentence or paragraph
cap	use a capital letter
frag	sentence fragment; incomplete sentence
gr	grammatical error
M? *or* nc	meaning is not clear
p	punctuation error
pron *or* ref	unclear pronoun reference; what does the word refer to?
rep	awkward repetition
r-o	run-on sentence
sp	error in spelling
t *or* vt	incorrect verb tense
ww	wrong word — choose a better one

_____   _____

_____   _____

_____   _____

_____   _____

_____   _____

_____   _____

_____   _____

Chapter 5

WRITER'S CHOICE: 105 IDEAS FOR EVERY KIND OF PAPER

During any school year, you will probably write a number of compositions. *Descriptive, narrative, expository,* and *persuasive* are terms which stand for the four main types of writing. Learning what each type consists of and how it can benefit your particular paper will add style and variety to every assignment you do — from single paragraphs to twenty-page term papers.

Although each type of writing will be discussed separately in this chapter, keep in mind that they frequently work together within a single composition. Description is very much a part of both narration and exposition; narrative writing is used at times to highlight expository and persuasive themes; and expository writing is often included in persuasive articles.

Following the explanation of each writing type are ideas that can be used to create a paper in that style. And, the last two sections of the chapter are devoted to two types of expository writing assignments dear to the hearts of every student — the essay test and the book report. After reading some A+ tips about these two feared (and sometimes hated!) compositions, perhaps you'll relax a bit more when the next one rolls around.

PICTURE THIS: DESCRIPTIVE WRITING

If you've got an eye for detail, descriptive writing should be a breeze. Writing a descriptive composition demands that a person look closely at the world and react to it intellectually and emotionally. The most necessary skill for this type of writing is the ability to use *all five senses* (sight, hearing, smell, taste, and touch) to observe and record your surroundings precisely. In a descriptive paper your aim is to create a picture of your subject in the mind of the reader. Naturally, the sharper and clearer this written picture is, the better the reader will be able to visualize exactly what you mean.

Some techniques that you can use to increase your reader's awareness and make your writing more descriptive are:

1. realistic details
2. specific, concrete language
3. vivid similes and metaphors

(For more on how to brush up on these techniques, see "Tell It Like It Is," in Chapter 3, page 60.)

The more observant you train yourself to be, the better word pictures you can "paint" for your readers. So, grab your "brushes" — here are some ideas for that next descriptive writing assignment:

Describe . . .
1. the first thing you saw when you woke up this morning
2. a fire
3. a stranger who walked past you today
4. love
5. a favorite meal
6. what it feels like to be bored or lonely
7. what happened fifteen minutes ago.
8. your family's car (*or* truck, motorcycle, boat, van, etc.)
9. the qualities desirable in a good friend
10. having a tooth drilled and filled
11. yourself
12. the sights, sounds, smells, and tastes associated with your favorite holiday
13. strange noises in the middle of the night
14. a favorite movie or television star
15. your room as you left it this morning

WHAT'S THE STORY? NARRATIVE WRITING

Since everyone likes a good story, it's no wonder that the narrative is such a popular form of writing. Fairy tales, anecdotes, short stories, novels, plays, comics, and even some poems are all examples of the narrative form. Simply stated, a narrative is a story based on fact *or* fiction.

Any type of narrative (or story) writing is built on a series of events. By telling about these events one after the other, just as they occurred, your story will satisfy a reader's curiosity about what happens next. (A more complex narrative device of moving back and forth from past to present within a story is called the *flashback* technique.)

A narrative composition can be used to entertain, make a point, and/or illustrate a premise. Whatever the purpose, you may want to experiment with developing characters, setting, mood, and dialogue. (If you use dialogue remember the basic rules — 1. everything actually being said is enclosed in quotation marks and, 2. always begin a new paragraph whenever a new character begins to speak.) You'll probably find as you write your story that you will rely on description to add color and life to the events. This is only one of the many ways in which the different forms of writing interact with one another.

If you can tell a story, you can write a story — or narrative — composition. Here is a list of ideas to get you started:

1. Trace your family tree, then write a story about one of your long-lost relatives. It may be fact or fiction.

2. Select a famous historical incident or event and write an account of it as if you were a participant.

3. Write a story to accompany a famous photograph, painting, or drawing.

4. Write an updated version of a well-known folk or fairy tale.

5. Write a story that takes place fifty years from now.

6. People-watch for an afternoon. Then write a story based on someone you spotted.

7. Take notes first thing in the morning about one of your dreams. Expand your notes into a fictional story.

8. Write about a day in the "life" of an inanimate object. (Suggestions: a mirror, football, quarter, refrigerator, rug, or paperclip.)

9. Build a story around the popular proverb, "Better late than never" (or any other proverb of your choice).

10. Write a story (in prose or poetry) appropriate for a very young child.

11. Write a short story or play using the people in your English class as the only characters.

12. Write some funny dialogue between a father (or mother) and his/her daughter (or son) who must explain why she/he is two hours past curfew.

13. Give yourself a role in your favorite TV show. Then write the story of the episode you are in.

14. Rewrite a comic strip story in the style of a factual news story.

15. Take an anecdote from your experiences and write it up in comic-strip format.

FACTS OF THE MATTER: EXPOSITORY WRITING

The purpose of expository writing is to communicate factual information in essay form. It demands interest in and knowledge of a subject, *plus* the ability to organize these facts and opinions in a logical way. Once you practice the different kinds of expository writing, you'll find it to be the most practical and useful skill you can master.

In general, there are three particular types of expository essays: exposition that *defines*, exposition that *informs*, and exposition that *explains*. Although one composition will very often contain all three types, it's a good idea to get acquainted with each separately.

Expository essays that define call for short or extended definitions to help both the writer and reader understand the meaning of a word. Depending on the length of your essay, you may choose to develop your definition by *examples*, *comparisons*, and/or *functions*. Try any one of the following:

A hibachi is _____

Bad luck is _____

Gourmet food is _____

A digital watch is _____

A greeting card is _____

Pride is _____

Ballet is _____

A shoelace is _____

Warmth is _____

Delinquency is _____

Time is _____

A potato chip is _____

A clown is _____

Summertime is _____

Superman is _____

Expository essays that inform tell a reader "everything he always wanted to know about _____." Included are such things as essay test answers, book reports, outside research papers, and lab experiments. Their purpose is to inform others about something they might not be familiar with. (Unless, of course, your reader is your teacher and the occasion is a test. In this case, he or she will be on the lookout for specific information to be included.) Here are some suggestions for informative essays. If you're not familiar with the subject, do some quick research.

Equal Rights Amendment

Your best friend

Skylab

4-H Clubs

Chiropractic

The Olympic winners

Censorship

Nuclear power

A person you admire

Juvenile crime in your town

Your part-time job

The latest fad

Roller skating

Chemical preservatives

The athletic teams at your school

For more information on essay tests and book reports, see the special sections at the end of this chapter, pages 106–113.

Expository essays that explain tell "how-to" do something in such a way that anyone who is not acquainted with the process can understand it. Try explaining:

How to bathe a dog

How to balance a checkbook

How to train a parakeet

How to perform a magic trick

How to fall in love

How to eat spaghetti

How to tell time

How to break a bad habit

How to drive a car

How to play basketball

How to get to your house from school

How to change a light bulb

How to choose a ripe melon

How to lose gracefully

How to wallpaper a room

POWERS OF PERSUASION: PERSUASIVE WRITING

There's no doubt that your personal opinion enters into many of the papers that you write. But a persuasive composition is built on opinion. In it you use your own experiences, thoughts, and/or impressions to make a point, convince someone about an idea, or debate one side of an argument or issue.

You can write an A+ persuasive paper if: 1. you have a good case, 2. you are thoroughly convinced of something, and 3. you present your beliefs in a well-organized, sincere manner. Probably the most important thing to remember about persuasive writing is to choose your words carefully and be alert to their connotative and denotative meanings. (See "Shades of Meaning," Chapter 3, page 63.) You also want to make your argument believable and here are three suggestions on how to do just that:

1. Cite facts to support your point of view. (Name the sources of these facts if there's a chance your readers might question them.)

2. Relate a personal experience or incident if it is relevant to the topic and supports your point of view. (Don't, however, throw in a story just for laughs or to take up an extra 150 words. If the incident has nothing to do with the point of your essay, save it for cafeteria conversation.)

3. Quote authorities who support your viewpoint. (Your Aunt Roberta, unless she's a doctor, might not be a good person to quote on a medical issue.) Certainly you can quote someone you know, but make sure that that person qualifies as an authority and will help you to convince your readers.

Get ready to practice your powers of persuasion. Here are some ideas:

1. Write a magazine advertisement to sell one

104

of the following items: last year's calendar; one shoe; a safety pin; string; crab grass.

2. Write an intelligent plea to your parents asking them to extend your curfew by two hours.

3. You hate the latest fashion in clothing. Write an essay telling why.

4. Enter an imaginary contest. Win an imaginary trip to Italy! Write a letter convincing the judges that you really adore Thinetti Spaghetti Strands.

5. Convince someone — in writing — to buy your used car.

6. Tell why or why not cigarette smoking should be against the law.

7. Write a letter persuading someone to lend you some money.

8. Write an essay telling why _____ should be President of the United States.

9. Write a paper convincing people that you really saw a UFO.

10. Imagine that you're running for mayor of your hometown. Write a campaign speech convincing the people that, "You're the One!"

11. Write an article telling the public that they should never watch TV again.

12. You are falsely accused of cheating on the final exam. Write a note to your teacher convincing her/him that you were not cheating.

13. Write an article for or against the death penalty.

14. Write a review of a local restaurant, convincing everyone to eat there.

15. Write a review of a book, convincing everyone not to read it.

TEST PATTERNS: A+ ESSAY TEST TIPS

An essay test requires you to demonstrate how well you understand the ideas presented in class, rather than simply stating a memorized fact. Answers may range from one paragraph to many pages, with the majority falling into the "few paragraphs" category.

The A+ tips that follow are based on the assumption that you have studied the material you're about to be tested on and that you do understand it. Believe it or not, lack of preparation is not the biggest cause of poor grades on essay tests. A lot of F's owe "thanks" to misinterpretation of the question, poor organization, and unclear expression of ideas. It's time to tackle those problems right now!

Your performance on any essay test is directly related to how well you understand what is expected of you. As in any written assignment, you should not begin until you're quite clear about where you're going with the material. Usually the wording of the question can provide you with a clue about how to organize the answer. Following is a "crash course" on "clue words" often found in essay test questions. Learn what they mean and you'll save yourself a lot of time when the pressure is on.

ANALYZE — Take it apart and determine what makes it work.

CITE — Mention or quote.

COMMENT ON — Discuss, criticize, or explain.

COMPARE — Examine two things and tell their similarities and differences.

CONTRAST — Examine two things and tell their differences.

COMPARE AND CONTRAST — Tell the similarities and differences between two things. Same as COMPARE.

CRITICIZE — Give your judgment or opinion of something. Show its good and bad points.

DEFINE — To tell what a word or a phrase means. This often requires memorizing a definition.

DESCRIBE — Present a detailed account or word picture in a logical sequence or story.

DIAGRAM — Make a graph, chart, or drawing and label it.

DISCUSS — Talk about a subject by carefully presenting various points with supporting evidence. Cover the pros and cons.

ENUMERATE — Name, list, and number the main ideas one by one.

EVALUATE — Give your opinion (or an expert's opinion) of the value of a concept. Tell the advantages and disadvantages.

EXPLAIN — Give the *reasons for* or *causes of* something.

ILLUSTRATE — Explain or make clear by using concrete examples, comparisons, or analogies.

INTERPRET — Explain the meaning of something.

JUSTIFY — State why you think something is so. Then give reasons for your statement or conclusion.

OUTLINE — Give a general summary. List only the main ideas (and some supporting ideas). Omit minor details.

PROVE — Show by argument or logic that something is true.

REVIEW — Summarize important parts and criticize.

STATE — Describe the main points in brief, clear sentences.

SUMMARIZE — Give a brief account of the main ideas. Omit details and examples. Similar to OUTLINE.

Once you fully understand what you are to do, it's time to get organized. But before you write even one word on your test paper be sure to take into account the period of time you have to work. Get organized by planning a rough time schedule. (Unless you can complete all the questions, your grade might suffer.) If your teacher assigns different point values to the various questions, obviously, you should spend more time on the ones worth the most points. Most teachers won't object to your answering the questions out of order as long as they are correctly numbered on your answer sheets.

To save time and get a higher score, outline what you want to say in the essay. You can do this on scratch paper, in the margin of the test paper, or, if you have a good memory, in your head. This by no means has to be a formal outline, just a listing of all the facts, names, dates, and examples you want to include. Check them off as you develop them within the essay.

Organize your answer so that the first paragraph gets directly to the point. Let your teacher know from the very beginning that you know what you are talking about. The rest of your essay should support and develop the topic statement with facts and examples.

When you've adequately covered the main points, stop and move on. You don't need to write extra paragraphs to prove your knowledge of the subject. Your teacher usually has a definite idea of what she or he expects the answer to include and, the sooner its mentioned, the better.

ON THE BOOKS: CREATIVE BOOK REPORT IDEAS

Do you love to read but cringe at the thought of writing another why-I-did-or-did-not-like-the-book assignment? Do you find that you write down *everything* that happened in the book to prove to your teacher that you read it? Do you consider a good report one that simply paraphrases the back cover copy? Well, if you're bored writing a book report, chances are your teacher will be bored reading it.

The book report is a special kind of essay because of all the options open to you. Any book report can be made into a paper that defines, informs, explains, persuades, and/or describes. It is clearly an opportunity to be creative. Take advantage of it!

Following is a list of ideas for really challenging and imaginative ways to present your book report. Hopefully, these ideas will encourage you to analyze and constructively criticize what you read, and you'll learn more from a book than just the author's name. These kinds of reports can be so much fun to write that you might even look forward to your next assignment. Just check with your teacher before beginning the assignment in case she or he has some specific guidelines not mentioned in this book.

1. You are an interior decorator. Design a new home for the main character(s) in your book. Choose a style that you think would best suit your "client," for instance, futuristic, Danish Modern, Early American, or French Provincial. Describe your plans in detail or draw pictures of them.

2. Create a new character for your book. Explain what he/she could add to the story in terms of other characters, plot, etc. At what point would you introduce this new personality? Rewrite a short section of the book, introducing your new character into the story.

3. You've been hired to produce a film for the book you have just read. Which contemporary stars would you cast as the various characters in this novel? Why? Discuss the physical and personality characteristics that make each star the most desirable person for a particular role. (If

your novel has already been made into a film, ignore the original cast and choose your own.)

4. Discuss the importance of setting in your novel. Bring in photographs and/or make a slide presentation of the areas featured in the book. Did this particular setting add to or detract from the story? Was it an integral part of the plot? Imagine you could change the setting — where could you envision the story taking place? Why?

5. As an astrologer you are well-acquainted with the different personality traits associated with the different birth signs. Choose the sign that best fits each of the major characters in your novel. Give reasons for your choices. If the book is non-fiction, give reasons why the personalities do or do not fit their actual signs.

6. Pretend you are a psychiatrist who has had several sessions with a character from your novel. The character has left your office and you are jotting down your notes. Share some pages of your notes that analyze the conflicts and problems of this particular character.

7. You are planning a party with a theme based on your novel. Describe your ideas for invitations and decorations as well as food and entertainment. If you're really ambitious, you might create samples of the invitations or some decorations. Explain what the theme is and specifically which characters will be invited.

8. You are out at a Chinese restaurant with the main characters from your book. On this particular night the fortune cookies are amazingly appropriate. Describe each character and tell what his or her fortune cookie said and why it's fitting.

Don't forget to include yourself!

9. Working with another student who has read the same book, develop a "Meet the Author" spot for a talk show. (For ideas you might want to tune in to such television shows as *Today*, *Good Morning America*, *Tonight*, or any local radio interview program.) One of you should assume the identity of the host/interviewer and the other that of the author. Both of you should work together in advance of your scheduled "appearance" to develop good questions. Most questions should apply specifically to the book; some may relate, however, to the author's personal life (information from the book jacket or a biography about the author will help you with this part).

10. Pretend you are a judge reviewing the case presented in your novel. What would be *your* verdict?

11. Design a series of comic strips which illustrate several scenes or themes from your book. Reproduce dialogue from the book itself or create new, appropriate dialogue to fit the sequences.

12. Pretend you are one of the judges for the Pulitzer Prize for Literature, an annual award honoring excellence in writing. Decide whether or not you would nominate the book you've just read for such an award. Then write a letter to the author explaining why you've accepted or rejected his or her work to compete for such high honors.

13. You are fixed up on a blind date with one of the characters from your book. You are thrilled when you open the door! Tell who is standing there and explain why you are so happy. Now

imagine that you are miserable when you open the door and feel like slamming it in this person's face. Who is it? Explain why you are so disappointed.

14. Your job is to design an ad campaign to promote your book. Think of ideas for a new cover, inside jacket, poster, window banner, and display carton. Sketch your ideas or put them together to form a display. You might want to present your ideas in the form of a sixty-second TV or radio commercial.

15. Imagine that you are a talented, sought-after screenwriter hired to develop a television mini-series based on your book. Decide what parts you are going to adapt for the "small screen" and describe what you will include, exaggerate, or drop entirely. Write a draft of the first episode which must introduce the characters and basic plot and make people want to tune in again next week.

CHARTING A WINNING COURSE: A PROGRESS CHART FOR COMPOSITIONS

This chart is provided as a way for you to keep track of your progress in writing. After reading over each paper that is returned to you, make a note of your teacher's comments about your composition's strengths and weaknesses. In the last column at the right, write a short reminder of what you'd like to work on in your upcoming papers.

Glance over this chart at the start of each new assignment. By refreshing your memory about previous strengths and weaknesses, you are less likely to make the same mistakes twice. And, as the school year progresses, take pride in watching these weaknesses turn into strengths.

Composition Title	Date	Teacher's Comments	Areas to Improve in Next Composition

Composition Title	Date	Teacher's Comments	Areas to Improve in Next Composition

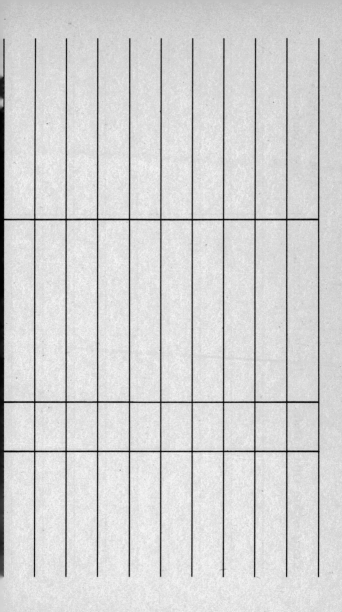

Composition Title	Date	Teacher's Comments	Areas to Improve in Next Composition

AFTERTHOUGHTS: A PERSONAL RECORD OF "WRITE" IDEAS

Some things to think about, such as . . . jokes, observations, questions, quotations, anecdotes, new words, favorite poems, snatches of conversations, ideas for stories, news items, character sketches, and anything else that comes to mind.

_____

_____

_____

_____

_____

_____

_____

_____

_____

_____

_____

INDEX

abbreviations, 72, 87
acronyms, 72

body of paper: *see* developmental paragraphs
book reports, 101, 102, 109–113
brainstorming, 6, 10

clichés, 69–70, 82
comments of teacher, 93–94, 114–119
conclusions, 48–50, 81
connective words and phrases, 39–42, 81
connotation: *see* words, connotation of
consistency of language, 71–73, 82
corrections on papers, 93–94, 114–119
    symbols for, 93–94

denotation: *see* words, denotation of
descriptive writing, 96–97
developmental paragraphs, 47–48
dictionaries, 6–7
drafts, 27–28, 28–29, 75–77, 78

editing: *see also* drafts; revisions, 75–77, 78–80
endings: *see* conclusions
essay tests, 101, 102, 106–109
essays: *see* essay tests; expository essays
expository essays, 100–103

facts, use of, 32–33, 36–37, 98, 100, 104
format of paper, 83

grammar: *see* language usage; punctuation;
    paragraphs, structure of; sentence structure

introductory paragraphs, 42–47, 48

jargon, 65–67, 67–69, 82
journal-writing, 5–6, 10, 120*ff.*

language usage, 55–56, 57–63, 65–67, 67–69, 69–70,
    71–74, 73–74, 82
libraries, 4–5, 11–12

mechanics of paper: *see* format of paper

narrative writing, 98–100

opening paragraphs: *see* introductory paragraphs
opinion, use of, 32–33, 36–37, 100, 103–105
organization
    of papers, 14–17, 18–23, 29–31, 32–35, 42–47,
        47–48, 48–50, 53, 81–82, 83
    tests and, 108–109
outlines
    essay tests and, 108
    papers and, 18–23, 48

paragraphs
    concluding, 48–50, 81
    developmental, 47–48
    introductory, 42–47, 48
    length of, 37
    structure of, 29–31, 32–35
persuasive writing, 103–105
proofreading, 78–80, 83
punctuation, 28, 87–92

question-asking, 7–8
quoting, 36, 46–47

reference sources, 6–7, 11

research, 11, 19, 101–102
revisions, 3, 27–28, 28–29, 75–77, 78–80, 80–82
rewriting: *see* drafts; editing; revisions

sentence structure, 28, 55, 56, 57–63, 82
spelling, 28, 82, 84–87
story writing: *see* narrative writing
study habits, 2, 3
structure: *see* paragraphs, structure of; sentence
    structure
style: *see* writing style
supplies, 3, 6–7, 83

test-taking: *see* essay tests
thesaurus, 6–7
thesis development, 14–17, 19–23, 42, 53
titles, 24–26
tone: *see* writing style
topic sentences, 29–31, 32–35, 37, 48, 81
topics
    choosing, 9–12
    developing, 14–17, 19–23, 53, 81
    narrowing, 13–14
transitional words and phrases, 38–40, 81
typing, 4, 75, 83

vocabulary improvement, 73–74

word games, 73–74
words: *see also* jargon
    connotation of, 63–65
    denotation of, 63–65
    usage of, 55–56, 57–64, 65–67, 71–73, 73–74, 82
work space, 2
writing
    style, 51–56, 57–63, 82
    types of, 95–96, 96–97, 98–100, 100–103, 103–105